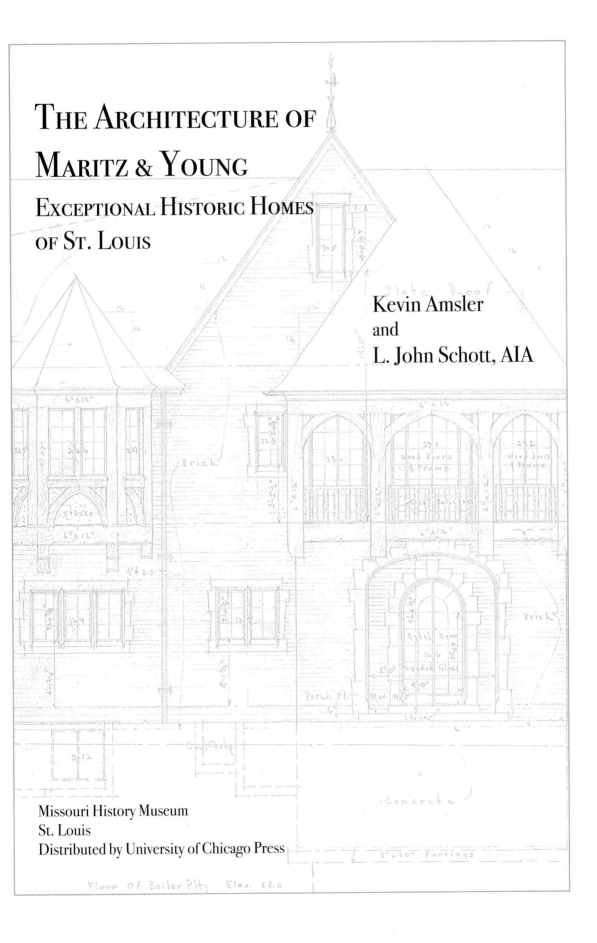

The Architecture of
Maritz & Young

Exceptional Historic Homes
of St. Louis

Kevin Amsler
and
L. John Schott, AIA

Missouri History Museum
St. Louis
Distributed by University of Chicago Press

Library of Congress Cataloging-in-Publication Data

Amsler, Kevin.

The architecture of Maritz & Young : exceptional historic homes of St. Louis / Kevin Amsler & L. John Schott, AIA.

pages cm

Includes bibliographical references and index.

ISBN 978-1-883982-76-8 (hardback)

1. Maritz & Young (Firm) 2. Maritz, Raymond E., 1893-1973--Themes, motives. 3. Young, Ridgely--Themes, motives. 4. Architecture, Domestic--Missouri--Saint Louis--History--20th century. 5. Saint Louis (Mo.)--Buildings, structures, etc. I. Schott, L. John. II. Title. III. Title: Architecture of Maritz and Young.

NA737.M21675A84 2013

728.092'2--dc23

2013016068

Cover image: Walter Hecker House, side elevation. Maritz & Young Collection, University Archives, Department of Special Collections, Washington University Libraries.

Back cover, top: Walter Hecker House. From Maritz & Young, Inc., *A Monograph of the Work of Maritz & Young*, Volume Two, 1930.

Back cover, bottom: Richard Waltke House, stair hall. From Maritz & Young, Inc., *A Monograph of the Work of Maritz & Young*, Volume One, 1929.

Back inside flap: W. Palmer Clarkson House, door detail. Maritz & Young Collection, University Archives, Department of Special Collections, Washington University Libraries.

Printed in the United States by Thomson-Shore, Inc.

Distributed by University of Chicago Press

TABLE OF CONTENTS

—⚒—

Foreword

THIS BOOK BEGINS WITH A DESCRIPTION of the Eugene Nims House on the bluffs overlooking the Mississippi River and the low-lying land in Illinois to the east. After the house was finished, I remember quite clearly going as a six-year-old member of the family to a lunch hosted by Mr. and Mrs. Nims to celebrate its completion. After an elegant meal during which Mrs. Nims wore one of her famous hats, my brother and I explored the bluff leading down to the river below while the Nimses and my parents talked.

Although I was too young to know why, I have always remembered the goodwill and good feeling of that lunch. In the years that followed, this feeling was renewed many times by others in spite of the lean years after the 1929 stock market collapse, World War II, and the postwar time spent rebuilding a career in a world that had changed.

During these difficult years—and they were difficult—my father was always good natured and optimistic, his lofty goals and qualities reflected in his work. He enjoyed life and loved France and anything French. He spoke three languages and loved to read. He was kind and generous. To borrow a phrase from Rudyard Kipling, he could "meet with triumph and disaster and treat those two impostors just the same."

I joined the architecture firm when it was rebuilding after World War II and the Korean War. Our work included churches, schools, commercial work, and institutional and office buildings. Near the end of his life, my father designed two beautiful homes, one for a fellow member of the American Field Service, Johnny Janes, whom he knew from World War I, and one for Ellis Brown, Johnny Janes's son-in- law. It was a fitting end to my father's career.

The practice of architecture keeps you young. Each new job starts with a client, a site, and a blank piece of paper. It was the same for the Janes House as for the Nims House many years earlier. Each one is unique, but the creative process is the same.

When you look at the photographs that follow, look for the love of life they reflect, the personality of the owner, the loving care of the craftsman, and the harmony of the landscape. My father used to say that if it is not offensive, it is already good. He was a modest man.

The homes and other work in this book represent a brief period in our history that is not likely to return. It was a hopeful and happy time. I am grateful to Kevin Amsler and John Schott for their effort to keep the memory of that time alive.

—*Raymond E. Maritz, Jr.*

As one drives into Bee Tree Park in south St. Louis County, the road leads up a slight incline, curving right to reveal a beautiful old stone house that seems out of place in an area of modern subdivisions. The house was commissioned by Eugene Nims as an elegant weekend retreat for his family. The residence sits majestically on a bluff above the Mississippi River as a beacon to the barge traffic plying the muddy waterway below. The house is engaging from every viewpoint: the rustic stone façade and gray slate roof of the front elevation, the overhanging timber sleeping porch on the side, and the two-story window bay extending from the rear. The house was designed by Maritz & Young, one of the most prominent St. Louis residential architectural firms during the 1920s and early 1930s.

One hundred years ago, Raymond Maritz began an architectural journey that resulted in the design and construction of an impressive collection of houses around the St. Louis area. His partnership with W. Ridgely Young established the firm's name and initiated two decades of work that transformed the St. Louis landscape. Many of the Maritz & Young houses were constructed in the stylish communities of Clayton, Ladue, and Huntleigh in St. Louis County and within the St. Louis city limits north of Forest Park, home of the 1904 World's Fair. Their portfolio contains over 150 prestigious houses commissioned by a collection of prominent citizens known for their corporate and civic leadership. Many of these homeowners were listed in the *St. Louis Exclusive Social Register*, a small, annually published directory of St. Louis notables. Today, these houses are fancied above most others, are bragged about in real estate listings, and sell for millions of dollars. More than seventy of the residences are listed in the National Register of Historic Places.

—ⵣ—

Raymond Maritz

The Eugene Nims House, 1929

The Architecture of Maritz & Young

The year was 1893. An economic panic was sweeping the country, businesses were collapsing, railroads filed for bankruptcy, and mortgages were foreclosed. The United States was facing the worst depression up to that point in its history. Amid this financial turbulence, Chicago was celebrating the World's Columbian Exposition, the White City dream of renowned architect Daniel Burnham and landscape architect Frederick Law Olmsted. Their Beaux-Arts designs emphasized a classic symmetry and grand luminosity. This French style of architecture would be repeated by American designers through the early twentieth century.

One of those architects influenced by the Beaux-Arts style and other European designs was Raymond Edward Maritz. Born in St. Louis on August 9 during the Panic of 1893, Maritz would become one of the most talented and sought-after residential architects in St. Louis. To Maritz, the commissions were not just houses, they were custom-designed sanctuaries; the owners were not mere clients but the beginnings of friendships that would last a lifetime. Many homeowners commissioned second houses or residential renovations and additions. Though his work was predominantly Tudor Revival in nature, Maritz also designed houses that ranged from Georgian Colonial to Spanish Eclectic to French Renaissance.

THE WALTER HECKER HOUSE, SIDE ELEVATION, 1927

And though he designed in traditional styles of the time, his plans are original; the drawings are crisp and lively, and many are exquisite works of art deserving of a gallery exhibit. These houses evoke prosperity, class, and elegance, whether the structure was a small cottage design or a prominent stone and brick mansion.

Raymond's father, Edward, ran the Maritz Jewelry Manufacturing Company that became the foundation for Maritz, Inc. Edward was born in New Orleans during the Civil War, in 1863. He was educated in St. Louis public schools before beginning a career as an apprentice with L. Bauman Jewelry Company. He later spent time in California learning the jewelry business before returning to St. Louis and Bauman Jewelry. Edward then moved to Kansas City to work as a manager for E. Jaccard Jewelry Company before joining another jewelry concern in Kansas City. He returned to St. Louis permanently in 1894 and established his own jewelry business. Within a decade, he incorporated E. Maritz Jewelry Manufacturing and moved to offices at N. Sixth Street in downtown.

Edward married Fannie Gilfoy in 1891. Besides Raymond, the couple had two other sons, James (1895–1981) and Lloyd (1899–1955), who would divide their father's expanded business, Lloyd taking over the jewelry division while

Edward Maritz family: Raymond, Lloyd, Fannie, Edward, and James

James ran the sales promotion. By 1921, Maritz Jewelry was located at 318 N. Eighth Street with Edward as president, James as vice president, and Lloyd as secretary-treasurer. It was the first American jewelry company to become a major importer of Swiss watch movements, and James was believed to be one of the first men in St. Louis to wear a wristwatch. James and his wife, Eugenia, lived in an Italian Renaissance–style house—designed by his brother Raymond—on Maryland Avenue before moving to another Maritz & Young design on Carrswold Drive. Edward Maritz died in 1929 when his son Raymond was at the height of his architectural career.

Raymond's interest in architecture was born during preparations for the 1904 St. Louis World's Fair when he accompanied his father to meet with architects and engineers who designed the French Pavilion, a structure modeled after the Grand Trianon at Versailles, France. The fifteen-acre grounds contained gardens, ponds, and sculptures. Raymond, who was eleven years old at the time, went on to study architecture at Washington University in St. Louis, where he served as an officer in the Architectural Society during his junior year. Before graduating, he headed to the École des Beaux-Arts (School of Fine Arts) in Paris for additional architectural training. The Paris school heavily influenced American architecture from 1880 to the early twentieth century, with notable alumni Daniel Burnham, Cass Gilbert, and the first American architect to attend the school, Richard Morris Hunt.

Raymond Maritz first established a partnership with a fellow Washington University architectural student named Gale Henderson. Henderson was born in St. James, Missouri, on September 11, 1890. In 1914, he was president of his sophomore class and a member of the same Architectural Society as Maritz. According to *The Hatchet*, Washington University's yearbook, Henderson was described as a "noise provoker and yell leader." By 1920, he was married with two daughters (a third daughter came later) and living in Webster Groves, a suburb of St. Louis. The Maritz & Henderson firm was located in the old Federal Reserve Bank Building in St. Louis. Two of their early houses, both Georgian Revivals constructed in 1915 and located only blocks apart, are the Roy Atwood House on Southmoor Drive and the exquisite Gustav Bischoff Jr. mansion on Forest Ridge. Both houses display a keen sense of detail and architectural charm that would be in evidence over the next twenty years. Maritz & Henderson were also commissioned with a few designs in the historic Parkview and Ames Place neighborhoods in University City.

GALE HENDERSON, 1914

THE ROY ATWOOD HOUSE, MARITZ & HENDERSON, 1915

About 1915, with World War I already raging in Europe, Maritz returned to his ancestral home of France to volunteer for what became known as the American Field Service (AFS) after the United States entered the war. He was responsible for transporting wounded French soldiers from the battlefield to field hospitals in nearby villages. Maritz said of his time in Europe:

> We station ourselves at a base post connected by telephone with the trenches. When someone is wounded we are notified and take our machines to the first aid stations, carrying the "blessés" [wounded] back to the field post. We have a splendid group of men in our section, including the editor of an Eastern paper, an artist, two architects, a college professor, a chemical engineer, and several student and business men. There are twenty-four in all.

Other members of the AFS included literary notables Ernest Hemingway, E. E. Cummings, and W. Somerset Maugham. The organization began in 1914 when Americans living in Paris volunteered their time as ambulance drivers for the American Hospital in the capital city. The service expanded with Americans participating in every major French battle by transporting more than 500,000 wounded soldiers. More than 2,500 Americans worked for the service. Maritz was awarded the Croix de Guerre (Cross of War) by the French government for his twenty-eight months of service.

Within a few years of returning to St. Louis, Maritz married Frances Duffett. Frances graduated from Washington University in 1916 and for several years was

LEFT: RAYMOND MARITZ WITH HIS WIFE, FRANCES, AND TWINS, RAYMOND JR. AND GEORGE
BELOW: THE MARITZ HOUSE ON WESTMORELAND DRIVE

THE CHEMICAL BUILDING

a teacher at Central Institute for the Deaf. The couple honeymooned in France where Maritz had an abiding love of the country and its architecture. They had three children, twin sons Raymond Jr. and George, and daughter Helen. During the 1920s and 1930s, the Maritz family lived on Westmoreland Drive in University City. Maritz designed the attractive Tudor brick and half-timber house in 1920.

Professionally, Maritz continued his partnership with Henderson. During this time, they opened an office in the Chemical Building at 721 Olive Street. The sixteen-story Chemical Building, built in 1895, became the offices of several architectural firms, including the city's largest firm, Mauran, Russell & Crowell. The office, even into the 1980s when the firm moved to a new location, had a medieval Old World charm with heavy arched doors, vaulted ceilings, and beautiful dark wood paneling throughout. The thick decorative conference table and its royal high-backed chairs were the predominant furnishings.

Gale Henderson left the firm in 1920 to join Angelo Corrubia, a graduate of Washington University and Massachusetts Institute of Technology (MIT). Among their projects, the duo designed several houses in Clayton before separating in 1926. Henderson established his own design-build firm and for the remainder of his career designed numerous grand residences in Clayton and Ladue, in addition to churches and public buildings. He died in 1969 of a heart ailment.

When Henderson left Maritz in 1920, Raymond established a new partnership with his office manager, W. Ridgely Young. They began their new association by designing a house on Maryland Avenue for Maritz's brother James. By 1929, the firm employed forty people.

William Ridgely Young was born in Louisville, Kentucky, to Walter and Anna Young on November 4, 1893, three months after Raymond Maritz was born. He worked as a draftsman for Mauran, Russell & Crowell in 1913. He attended Washington University before studying a short time at the American E. F. Art Training Center in Bellevue, France. He enlisted in the army in September 1917 and left for France the following June, serving as a second lieutenant in the infantry. His

W. Ridgely Young in World War I uniform, and with his wife, Elizabeth, in 1921

World War I draft card describes a tall and slender architecture student with gray eyes and dark hair. He was living with his sister Helon Reichardt on Longfellow Boulevard at the time, in a house he designed in 1914.

After returning home, Young married Elizabeth Nulsen on June 15, 1921. Elizabeth repeatedly referred to her husband in her diary, first as fun-loving "Brigham," then affectionately as "Itchie." They honeymooned in Europe, exploring the architectural wonders of Paris, the Loire Valley, Madrid, Barcelona, Rome, and Venice. The couple had two daughters, Elizabeth and Helon, born in 1922 and 1925, respectively. In his free time Young enjoyed playing golf, fishing, reading, and gardening. Beyond working in the office, Maritz and Young and their wives also socialized quite often, according to Elizabeth's diaries.

Both Maritz and Young were members of the American Institute of Architects from 1924 to 1935. They were well respected, charming, and had a contagious love of detail in their designs. Their originality melded with traditional functional styles to form plans and elevations that displayed their artistic personalities. The ornamental detail and craftsmanship were ever present, from decorative towers and chimneys to half-timber façades. Their interiors often had elaborate staircases with classic wrought-iron railings. Many of the plans incorporated servants' or maids' quarters, a practice often followed by the upper-class house designs at the time. Maritz and Young were known for remaining faithful to their contractors. Most residences were built by J. M. Higbee Construction; other contractors

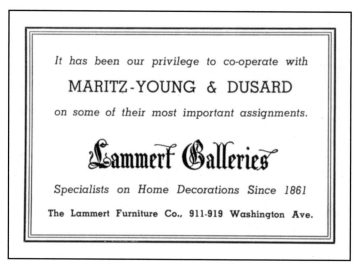

ONE OF THE FIRMS MARITZ & YOUNG USED FAITHFULLY

included Sauerbrunn Construction (brickwork), Reitz Brothers Stone Company (masonry), Geo. A. Riddle & Company (slate and tile roof), Volk Brothers Iron Works (ornamental iron), and Arthur Giroland & Company (terrazzo). The skill of the craftsmen at these firms contributed to the reputation Maritz & Young had for high quality.

Their business exploded in the 1920s with a large number of commissions. While Bobby Jones was accumulating golf championships from 1923 to 1930, Maritz and Young were designing and constructing an extraordinary collection of residences. These picturesque houses are as remarkable as the clients they sheltered. The homes range from the French Renaissance splendor of hotel owner Morris Corn's mansion to Henry Friedman's colorful Tudor Revival beauty to Young's own modest Spanish-style abode. Maritz & Young houses dominated stylish boulevards and drives with names such as Lindell, Forsyth, Carrswold, and West Brentmoor. Their work also includes institutional designs for the United Hebrew Temple (current home to the Missouri History Museum's Library and Research Center) and clubhouses for Bridlespur, Hillcrest, and Westwood country clubs. For the temple project, Maritz & Young consulted with architect Gabriel Ferrand, whom the pair certainly had known during their time at Washington University. Ferrand was named dean of the Washington University School of Architecture in 1916.

The firm published the first volume of *A Monograph of the Work of Maritz & Young* in 1929, with a second volume the following year. Most of the photographs in this book are taken from these volumes. The firm's architectural philosophy was stated in the beginning of each volume:

MARITZ & YOUNG MONOGRAPH, 1929

THIS ISSUE PRESENTS A SELECTION OF THE WORK

DESIGNED IN THE OFFICES OF

MARITZ, YOUNG & DUSARD, Inc.

ARCHITECTS

SAINT LOUIS, MISSOURI

ARCHITECTURE AND DESIGN MAGAZINE, 1939

> Every residence illustrated in this monograph represents a solution of
> the various problems involving the combination of a practical and artistic
> adaption to the site; and an interior arrangement which harmonizes both
> the personality and complete requirements of the owner.

The Depression years were difficult for the firm; commissions dried up, and construction slowed or halted entirely. Maritz & Young's fortunes improved as the
economy gained ground in the mid-1930s. Houses for Leo Carton in Huntleigh and
Fred Hermann in Ladue were completed, as well as commercial projects for the
Candle-Light House restaurant in Richmond Heights and Clayton National Bank.

Another change occurred when the firm added a third partner. Rime Dusard
joined Maritz & Young in 1934. He was born in St. Louis on July 8, 1895; his
Belgian father, Jean Baptiste, owned the North St. Louis and Wabash Transfer
Company as well as the Dickman-Dusard Seed Company. Rime Dusard served
in World War I as a sergeant in the 128th Field Artillery of the United States
Army. In June 1920, he married Bernadine Robertson; the couple would have two
daughters. While attending Washington University, Dusard was a member of the

Architectural Society and graduated from the School of Architecture in 1927.

A monthly publication called *Architecture and Design* devoted an issue in 1939 to Maritz, Young & Dusard's work. The volume included not only residential projects but also their commercial and institutional work, such as Clayton City Hall, Donnelly Mortuary, and St. Agnes Home for the Aged. Dusard left the firm in the mid-1940s. He was president of the Home Builders Association of Greater St. Louis in 1948. He was living in University City when he died from complications of a stroke in 1966.

When America's involvement in World War II began with the attack on Pearl Harbor, Maritz went to Washington, D.C., where he was placed with the Office of Strategic Services (OSS), predecessor of the Central Intelligence Agency (CIA). He transferred to Rome following its liberation, where, associating with the British Foreign Office, he worked as a political observer for the rebuilding of the country. He received the French Legion of Honor for his service.

After two years of service, he returned to St. Louis and resumed the profession of architecture in his Chemical Building office. In 1948, Maritz was joined by his twin sons, Raymond Jr. and George, both graduates of the architecture program at MIT. George passed away in 1962 at the age of thirty-nine.

Raymond Jr. had first gone to MIT in 1939. He joined the Reserve Officers' Training Corps in 1941 and was placed into active duty after the attack on Pearl Harbor. He returned to MIT after the war to finish his architectural program. Later, during the Korean War, the army utilized his architectural background to employ him with a forty-man army group of Japanese architects and engineers in Tokyo. He spent twenty months in Japan.

W. Ridgely Young separated from the firm shortly before the war to go into business for himself. Divorced from his wife, Elizabeth, in 1929, he was living back at his sister's home on Longfellow Boulevard. On December 2, 1948, Young died at the age of fifty-five of a liver ailment.

The firm's name was changed a final time in 1948 to Raymond E. Maritz & Sons Architects, Inc. Their projects during this time involved modest residential work, from simple renovations to new construction, and an increased amount of commercial work (schools, churches, and institutional and office buildings), including Seven Holy Founders in Affton, Annunziata School in Ladue, and the Herbert Hoover Boys Club, located on the site of Sportsman's Park at Grand and Dodier. The office accepted both residential and commercial work from outside the St. Louis region, especially around the Midwest, but also as far away as California and even residential work in Johannesburg, South Africa. Maritz was described in a 1966 story in the *St. Louis Globe Democrat* as "a man of average height, with grey hair and mustache. He is soft-spoken, quiet-mannered and very reluctant to talk about himself." Raymond Maritz continued to work in his final days. He died in his Ladue home on June 9, 1973, at the age of seventy-nine. His wife, Frances, passed away five years later.

Raymond Jr. went on to run the firm until he retired and closed the office in 2006. He was the architect for the Maritz, Inc., campus in Fenton, Missouri, as well as the Wells Fargo Advisors (originally A. G. Edwards) complex at Jefferson Avenue and Market Street in downtown St. Louis. He also followed his father's footsteps in designing several distinctive houses, including modern lakefront homes at the Lake of the Ozarks in southwest Missouri.

The Washington University School of Architecture established the Raymond E. Maritz Professorship to honor the contributions of an architect whose work continues to inspire and display itself in and around the St. Louis area.

Architectural Styles of Maritz & Young

Maritz & Young—as well as Maritz & Henderson, and Maritz, Young & Dusard—incorporated several different architectural styles in their residential designs. Between the English style of the 1915 Maritz & Henderson houses to the French styles used by late-1930s designs with Dusard, the firm's architecture also included Tudor Revival, Norman, Georgian, and Spanish.

The most prominent influence on Raymond Maritz and W. Ridgely Young was Tudor Revival. This style takes references from the late Gothic era in England at the time of the ruling Tudor dynasty. Constructed of either stone or brick, these often rambling country houses include four-centered arches, heavy tim-

The Tudor Revival style (T. Lewin House)

THE NORMAN STYLE (ARNOLD STIFEL HOUSE)

bers, carved barge boards, and highly pitched roofs. Massive chimney stacks, sometimes terminating in individual decorative brick shafts, are featured along with leaded glass windows arranged in multiple groupings in both vertical walls and decorative bays. On the interior, large fireplaces, stone floors, rich wood paneling, and monumental staircases are distinctive design elements.

The Norman style is a hearkening back to French Normandy with its picturesque compositions. Steep roofs, small cornices, and towers—round, square, or octagonal—characterize this style. Stone or pattern brickwork is utilized much of the time with a possible whitewash finish lending an aged appeal. Stucco or pattern brick infill combined with half-timber work adds character to the overall design. Casement windows prevail, with painted solid shutters framing the openings.

The Georgian Revival house characterizes the English style of design prevalent during the reign of the Georges. Symmetrical exterior design belies the

THE GEORGIAN REVIVAL STYLE (KENNETH DAVIS HOUSE)

symmetry of the basic floor plan based around a central hall. The house is generally constructed of brick, many times in a Flemish bond (an ornamental style of bricklaying). Tall windows with many individual panes are arranged in a formal pattern. Entrance doors are paneled and surrounded by fluted pilasters supporting a cornice or pediment above. Interiors include classical motifs with stairs that are usually delicate in design.

The Mediterranean style is a blending of designs, usually more so of Italian and Spanish influences. In the Italian influence, a smoother stucco finish may be utilized with fewer openings piercing the wall. Roofs are composed of clay tiles. Entrance doors are richly paneled; full-length casements can be found at both first and second floors with low wrought-iron railings guarding the openings. Loggias also can appear at either floor level. The Spanish influence will also have stucco walls but with a rougher, whitewashed finish. Clay tile roofing rises above a rambling elevation evoking what *Modern Homes: Their Design and Construction*

The Mediterranean style (S. Watts Smyth House)

called "intended carelessness in design and execution." The house is generally lower set. Windows are deeply recessed and sometimes located behind pierced screens. On the interior, brilliant tiles are used as an ornamental element.

THE RESIDENCES OF
MARITZ & YOUNG

St. Louis, Missouri

Lindell Boulevard

While most of the houses designed by Maritz & Young are located in St. Louis County, the architects completed a few commissions within the city limits, predominantly on Lindell Boulevard.

The Catlin Tract was an area bounded on the north and south by the Forest Park Parkway and Lindell, and by Union and Skinker on the east and west. The land was purchased in 1901 by the Parkview Realty and Improvement Company with the expectation of use during the World's Fair in 1904. As expected, the Louisiana Purchase Exposition Company leased the land as the location for the Pike, a mile-long amusement district made up of rides, dancers, musicians, and concessionaires selling snacks and souvenirs. The land was subdivided after the fair for residential development.

As we stand on the sidewalk on the northern boundary of Forest Park west of the Jefferson Memorial, the first Maritz & Young project is the **Louis Monheimer House**. Set back from the street, this 1926 Tudor Revival exudes a country charm utilizing a variety of window sizes and groupings. Brick predominates in the elevations with stone trim and non-fussy details such as corbels and a carved panel above the two-story bay. The three arched openings of the loggia along the street façade are framed by the two gabled bays. Above the driveway a timber and stucco bay projects out from the second floor, supported by massive timber brackets. The attached garage roof with its brick and stone dormers stretches upward to match the roof peak of the main house.

A sweeping circular staircase gracefully leads up to the second floor from the main stair hall. The vaulted loggia connects the living room to the rest of the first floor. The arched openings seen on the façade are matched by duplicate open-

The Louis Monheimer
House living room
(above), stair hall and
stair hall detail (left
and above left), and
front (below)

The Residences of Maritz & Young

ings on the garden elevation that lead to outdoor terraces on both the front and rear of the residence. Beyond the loggia, through another arched opening, is the well-proportioned living room. This room features a decorative plaster ceiling and cornice, wood-paneled walls, built-in bookcases, a stone fireplace, and a bay at the front. Returning to the main stair hall, the dining room opens up to the left and likewise has a decorative plaster ceiling and cornice with wood-paneled walls.

On the second floor, a large master suite spans both the loggia and the living room below. This suite includes a marble fireplace, a bath and dressing room, its own sleeping porch, and access to a second bath. The drawings list a "burglar switch" located along one wall. Two other bedrooms and a bath complete the family's needs. A sewing room and two maids' rooms and a bath are located over the garage. Tucked away in a wall of the second-floor service corridor is a laundry chute to the basement. In the attic, there is a cedar closet with built-ins for clothing storage.

Louis Monheimer was a vice president for twenty years at May Department Stores, parent company of Famous-Barr. Though he was not a native, Monheimer lived in St. Louis for over thirty years. He was a member and vice president of Westwood Country Club. He sold his Maritz & Young house and later lived at the nearby Park Plaza Hotel. His family had a winter house in Miami where Monheimer died of pneumonia in 1939.

Continuing down Lindell toward Skinker Boulevard, the next Maritz & Young creation is the **Morris Corn House**. Corn was born in 1882 in Poland. He served as president of the St. Regis Hotel and the Palmer House Company, as well as the secretary-treasurer of the New Plaza Hotel Company; he later owned the Shelby Hotel. Corn and his wife, Marjorie, sold their Lindell mansion after the 1929 market crash. They were living in a house on Washington Terrace at the time of his death in 1946.

As with the Monheimer house, the Morris Corn residence was built in 1926. It is a very striking residence with a strong French influence. The symmetrical street façade in cut stone suggests the elegant interiors within. A prominent Renaissance-inspired dormer with large third-floor windows extends down to a second-floor balcony with a wrought-iron scrollwork railing, all set above an arched entranceway framed by quoins (large stones at the corners) and voussoirs (wedge-shaped stones). Multiple French doors allow light into both the first- and second-floor spaces.

THE RESIDENCES OF MARITZ & YOUNG

THE MORRIS CORN HOUSE.
FACING PAGE: FRONT
(ABOVE) AND DINING ROOM.
THIS PAGE: LOGGIA (ABOVE)
AND BEDROOM.

A center hall plan reveals graceful marble stairs with a delicate wrought-iron railing rising up to the second floor, backlit by a two-story bank of windows. Marble floors are featured in the overall floor design. From the main hall, archways open onto the elegant paneled living room. Decorative plasterwork compliments the carved wood pilasters and French-inspired fireplace. A sunroom lies off the living room with a beautiful vaulted ceiling and marble features, including a backdrop above a fountain pool. Across the main hall, the paneled dining room is crowned by another unusually decorated ceiling design. Adjacent to the dining room, an intimate breakfast room lies below a vaulted ceiling accentuating the two arched openings to the exterior.

Several houses past Des Peres Avenue on Lindell Boulevard sits the **Frederick Meyer House**. The book *Modern Homes: Their Design and Construction* describes this house as "adapting Spanish and Italian forms of architecture to the larger type of residence yet securing a thoroughly modernized American home." This Spanish-style residence seems out of place in its location, perhaps better suited to a Mediterranean hillside. The modest-sized (for Maritz & Young) house has a stucco exterior with shuttered windows on the second floor. The front door is surrounded by stonework with a fan-shaped wrought-iron grille and lantern above. All of the first-floor windows have glass fan transoms. A wide chimney rises to the right of a recessed covered wooden balcony.

The circular stair at the back of the main hall has varied design tiles on the risers and seems to have no means of support. The ironwork railing gives the stairs a classic feel. The sunken living room has a large fireplace along the front wall. The two-car garage extends from the back past the pantry. This seven-bedroom house includes three servants' rooms over the garage.

THE FREDERICK MEYER HOUSE

In 1952, sixty-year-old Frederick Meyer collapsed and died of a heart attack while playing golf at Glen Echo Country Club. He had worked for several companies during his career, including Hyde Park Breweries Association, Granite City Steel Company, and Richter Spring Corporation. He and his wife, Marie, were still living in their Lindell house at the time of his death.

Three doors down, the 1929 **Morton Jourdan House** is a very elegant French Regency–style residence in cut limestone. The front elevation is a composition in symmetry with its first-floor arches, French doors, and wrought-iron and stone balconies. Details include stone keystones, quoins, and balusters at the parapet. A porte-cochere to the left is balanced by the projecting sunroom to the east of the central bay. To the rear, beyond public view, beige brick is used in lieu of stone.

Entry is under the porte-cochere into the vaulted main hall, stretching directly ahead with a gleaming terrazzo floor extending to the vaulted sunroom. On the left, a circular stairway descends from above, while on the right, two openings with decorative wrought-iron gates access the living room spanning the central front bay. Five pairs of French doors are set into eighteen-inch-deep openings, allowing a generous amount of daylight to fill the space. Walls are paneled with walnut up to an ornamental plaster cornice. A fireplace is located at one end of the long axis. Across the hall, the formal dining room displays painted paneling. A pantry

THE MORTON JOURDAN HOUSE, FRONT ELEVATION

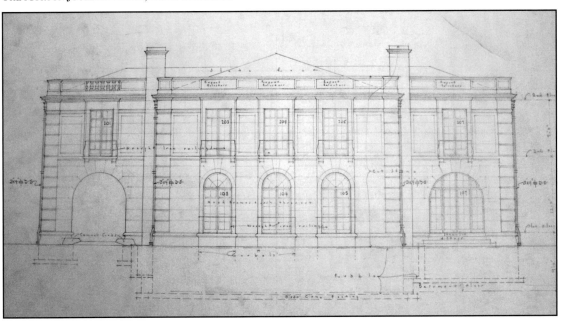

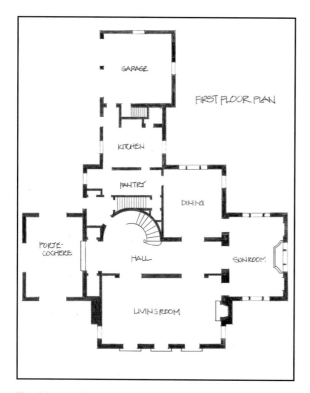

THE MORTON JOURDAN HOUSE, FIRST FLOOR PLAN

and kitchen continue to the rear side of the residence. An attached two-car garage projects beyond, into the garden.

Two light wells behind stained-glass panels illuminate the main stair. Three bedrooms and three baths lead from the second-floor vaulted hall. Painted wainscoting, wood molding, and plaster cornices carry throughout the bedrooms and baths with a fireplace highlighting the master suite.

Morton Jourdan was a corporate lawyer at Jourdan & English with offices in downtown St. Louis. He passed the bar in 1883 at the age of nineteen after apprenticing in a law office in Chillicothe, Missouri. He came to St. Louis in 1897 to establish his legal practice and went on to become president of the Missouri Bar Association. The *Encyclopedia of the History of Missouri* wrote of him, "He has built up an extensive and remunerative practice, and come to be known as one of the most continually occupied and successful lawyers in St. Louis." Jourdan's claim to local fame is that he is considered one of the first people in the city to own an automobile; for years he had license plate no. 1. Besides the Lindell house, he and his wife, Lara, also had a summer house in Minnesota. The Lindell house was later purchased by Arnold Stifel after he sold his Maritz & Young house in Ladue (see page 141).

Next door, the **Herman Schnure House** was built a mere twelve years after the St. Louis World's Fair. It was the work of Maritz & Henderson, before Young joined the firm. The home's ink-on-linen drawings may be the most beautiful of the designs from the next twenty years. This modest house has a grand appearance; the façade is long and squat with brickwork on the main floor and panels of brick separated by wood members on the second story. Two columns define the recessed entrance porch.

The floor plan steps back three times for the sunroom, breakfast room, and kitchen and garage at the back of the house. The residence has oak flooring

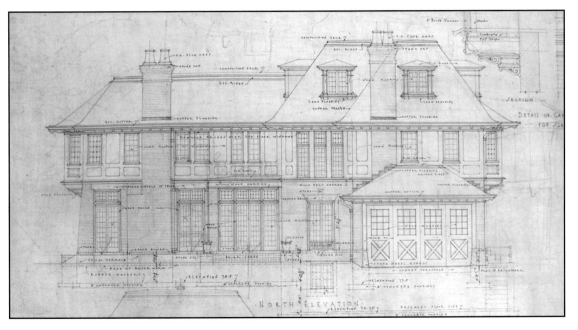

THE HERMAN SCHNURE HOUSE, GARDEN (ABOVE) AND FRONT ELEVATIONS

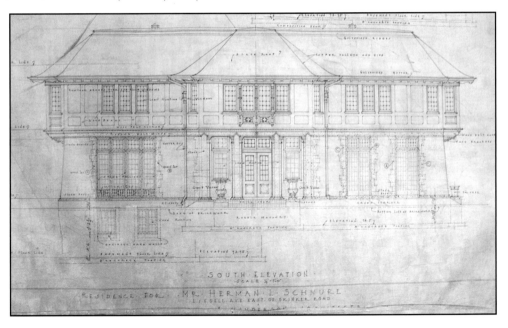

throughout except for yellow pine in the kitchen and pantry area. The four-bedroom, three-bath second floor also contains a sleeping porch. A smaller third-floor area on the left side of the home has two additional bedrooms and baths, and a children's playroom.

Herman Schnure was born in Pennsylvania and came to St. Louis in 1904 to work at the World's Fair. He later sold automobiles, such as the Pierce-Arrow, before becoming a pioneer Buick and Chevrolet dealer. He and his wife, Mildred, married at her family residence a short distance down Lindell Boulevard. By 1940, the family moved from Lindell to a Waterman Boulevard address.

The third Maritz & Young house in a row is the **Frank Alewel House**. The residence was built in 1929, the same year as the Morton Jourdan House. Frank Alewel (1884–1972) was born in St. Louis to Peter and Augusta Alewel, both natives of Germany. He first owned a furniture store before managing a loan company bearing his name. The company, located on Market Street downtown, dealt in real estate and loans. Alewel and his second wife, Ida, had one daughter.

With its three street-side gables, the façade is not symmetrical but displays a very balanced composition through creative window detailing. The central entrance bay of this Tudor Revival contains an arched, glassed-in vestibule below a stone and brick oriel. Instead of using bracket fixtures, lampposts at either side

THE FRANK ALEWEL HOUSE

THE RESIDENCES OF MARITZ & YOUNG

THE FRANK ALEWEL HOUSE, LIVING ROOM

of the vestibule frame the entrance. To the left of the entrance, a projecting bay at the first floor is situated under the smallest of the gables. Inset in the gable is a decorative carved stone panel. Three stone obelisks or finials highlight the parapet. The living room is a classic English interpretation with its decorative plaster ceiling, simple wood-paneled design, and fine carved stone fireplace.

FRANK ALEWEL

A Glimpse: Photographer LeRoy Robbins

Many of the photographs used in this book were taken in the 1920s by LeRoy S. Robbins. He was born in St. Louis in 1904 to LeRoy and Adelia Robbins. His father, also born in St. Louis, was educated at Washington University, studying mechanical engineering, and went on to become vice president of St. Louis Well Machine and Tool Company.

Robbins studied engineering in the mid-1920s at Washington University before entering the School of Architecture. He left school early and in time opened  his own photography studio. The 1930 *St. Louis City Directory* listed his business as LeRoy Robbins Architectural and Aerial Photography Company, with offices on Delmar Boulevard. Within a short time, he was the official photographer for the City Art Museum (now known as the Saint Louis Art Museum).

In 1931, Robbins spent nine months crossing Mexico on a botany photography trip. He relocated to Southern California, marrying Florence Sibilio of Santa Maria in November 1932. His camera led him to Hollywood, where he began taking still shots for the movie studios. In 1937, Robbins became a member of the Works Progress Administration (WPA) Federal Art Project. President Franklin D. Roosevelt's Depression-era program employed painters, sculptors, poster and graphic artists, photographers, and muralists to produce works, some for display in art centers and galleries the Federal Art Project opened across the country. That same year, he co-directed and co-starred with friends in a twelve-minute short called *Even: As You and I*.

In the 1940s, Robbins produced films for various government agencies and a decade later began working on sound recordings for motion pictures, including the 1969 classic *Easy Rider*. He reawakened his photography career in the early 1960s with shots incorporating an abstract flavor with an architectural influence. As a leading member of the California community of professional photographers, he was friends with other masters such as Ansel Adams and Edward Weston, his mentor. Robbins passed away in 1987.

Clayton, Missouri

Maritz & Young produced their most exquisite design work in St. Louis County, primarily in Clayton, Ladue, and Huntleigh. The houses would increase in square footage and grow more expensive as the architects worked on properties farther from the city limits where large lots were common. We'll begin our tour in Clayton.

Ralph Clayton came to Missouri about 1820 and purchased over six hundred acres approximately eight miles west of the riverfront. He lived on this land for the rest of his life, first residing in a two-story log house near present-day Clayton Road and Brentwood Boulevard. When this house burned down, he replaced it with a large brick home. Clayton worked as a farmer, tanner, and shoemaker during his lifetime. He was a warm and caring man, a teetotaler, and a pillar of his church. According to Dickson Terry in *Clayton: A History*, his home was "an open house to his friends and a haven for the less fortunate who might knock on his door." He married his neighbor's daughter, Rosanna McCausland, in 1831. Other friends and neighbors included recognizable names such as Martin Hanley, John McKnight, Robert Forsyth, and Thomas Skinker. Clayton died in 1883 at the age of ninety-five.

Ralph Clayton donated land for a new town and asked that the town be named for him. While he was still alive, the town of Clayton was formed with the laying of the cornerstone for a new courthouse. When a new city hall was dedicated in 1931, architect Raymond Maritz handed over the keys of his new Maritz & Young building to Clayton's mayor.

Maritz & Young houses occupy over seventy plots in Clayton, predominantly in Brentmoor Park, and on Carrswold Drive and Forsyth Boulevard.

West Brentmoor Drive

Brentmoor or West Brentmoor Drive (as labeled on the Maritz & Young drawings) in Clayton consists of nearly fifty acres laid out in 1913 by architect and landscape designer Henry Wright. Wright (1878–1936) studied at the University of Pennsylvania between stints as a draftsman for Root & Siemens, a Kansas City architectural firm. He then worked for the St. Louis office of George Kessler, once an employee of the great landscape designer Frederick Law Olmsted, and at the time chief landscape architect for the St. Louis World's Fair. Wright started his own practice in 1909. He had designed the related Brentmoor Park and Forest Ridge subdivisions immediately to the east three years earlier and had designed four of the houses there. The entire ensemble, including West Brentmoor Drive, is listed in the National Register of Historic Places.

In laying out his design for Brentmoor Park, Forest Ridge, and West Brentmoor, Wright situated the plots so that the houses would face inward toward common grounds and away from busy Wydown Boulevard. Wright also designed

STREETCAR PAVILION FRONTING WEST BRENTMOOR DRIVE

THE ARCHITECTURE OF MARITZ & YOUNG

Southmoor Drive and the grounds of the St. Louis Country Club in Ladue; both are locations of several Maritz & Young houses. Square stone pavilions, originally used by riders of the streetcar line, still frame Wydown Boulevard at the entrance to the neighborhood.

Maritz & Young designed ten houses on West Brentmoor Drive, all constructed between 1923 and 1929. Another architect who contributed to Brentmoor was Ernest Klipstein, who designed three houses, including his own home. Klipstein was also the architect for several Anheuser-Busch projects such as the Bevo Plant at the brewery, the Grant's Farm Bauernhof, and the Bevo Mill on Gravois Avenue.

Prominent residents of Brentmoor Park (though not living in Maritz & Young houses) were Morton J. May and his son Morton D. May, who both ran May Department Stores, the owners of Famous-Barr. Rival department store Stix, Baer & Fuller had its own Brentmoor resident in J. Arthur Baer II.

Note: Brentmoor is a private drive and, out of respect for the privacy of the residents, should not be toured.

—⅏—

As one enters the subdivision, the **Woodson Woods House** is on the right. This 1924 house gives a sense of English rustic sophistication with its artistic combination of stucco, stone, and slate with brick and timber details. The entrance façade follows the curve of the street as the vaulted living room wing angles from

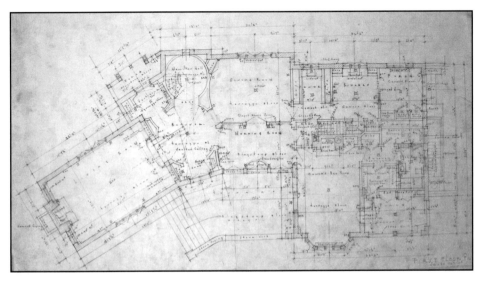

THE WOODSON WOODS HOUSE, FIRST-FLOOR PLAN

THE WOODSON WOODS HOUSE, GARDEN VIEW. INSET: WOODSON WOODS.

the main two-story body of the house. A timber porch with turned wood posts identifies the main entry. The garden side of the house features a timber balcony extending off the guest bedroom while an open sleeping porch is located above the master bedroom. A generous elevated stone terrace is situated outside the morning room. Continuing on, a three-car garage with two bedrooms and a bath above is connected to the main house by a covered gallery.

Woodson Woods was born in Kentucky and began his career as an office boy for J. B. Sickles Saddlery Company in St. Louis, followed by a few years as a bookkeeper at St. Louis Dairy Company. Woods became secretary and treasurer for Robinson Forage Company before joining Ralston Purina in 1895. Within fifteen years, he was executive vice president and treasurer. He was active in the business community as a director of the St. Louis Merchants' Exchange and on the board of both the YMCA and the YWCA. Woods retired in 1942 due to poor health but stayed on as a director. He passed away at home in February 1950, at the age of seventy-eight. His wife, Elizabeth, had died twenty-one years earlier. Living next door to Woods was his boss, Donald Danforth, an executive and the son of Ralston Purina's founder.

Upon entering the vaulted rotunda, one sees the barrel-vaulted living room that steps down to the right, the garden side terrace that lies ahead, and to the

THE ARCHITECTURE OF MARITZ & YOUNG

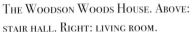
THE WOODSON WOODS HOUSE. ABOVE:
STAIR HALL. RIGHT: LIVING ROOM.

left, the morning room, dining room, and main stair. This house's layout is unique in that the master bedroom and bath are found on the first floor along with a private enclosed porch. On the second floor, a guest bedroom with its adjacent bath overlooks the living room. There are two more bedrooms and a bath for the children, and two servants' rooms and a bath over the service area.

Around the curve to a small cul-de-sac is another residence constructed in 1924, the **S. Watts Smyth House**. Sylvester Watts Smyth had the house constructed on the next lot east of his father's house. The original cost of the resi-

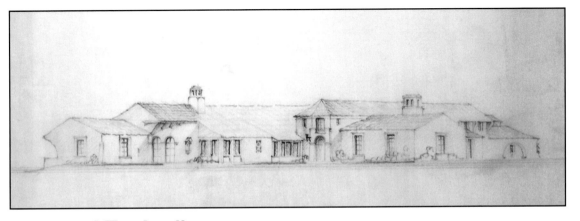

DRAWING OF THE S. WATTS SMYTH HOUSE

The S. Watts Smyth House (also pictured on page 24). Top: garden view.
Below: addition, 1935.

dence was approximately $22,000. His wife's parents also lived in Brentmoor
Park. Smyth studied mechanical engineering at Washington University before
running a realty company named for him. He and his wife, Jane, married in 1921
and honeymooned in Hawaii. They parented two daughters and later retired to
Wyoming.

The white stucco walls, clay tile roof, and second-floor balcony above the
entrance hearken back to a Spanish Colonial influence. The scale of the house
is not overwhelming. The plan was straightforward and even reminiscent of W.

Ridgely Young's own residence profiled later in this book. The story-and-a-half living room opens up from the stair hall with an overlook at the second floor revealing the exposed wooden roof structure. A dining room, pantry, kitchen, and radio room, along with two small maids' rooms and a bath, complete the main floor. A large rambling addition was designed in 1935, including two additional bedrooms and baths, circular stairs, a reoriented kitchen, a new breakfast room, and a four-car garage with an apartment above.

The main portion of West Brentmoor Drive resembles a thoroughbred racetrack. Outside the second turn entering the back stretch sits the **Walter Hecker House**. Hecker was born across the Mississippi River in Illinois in 1880. He was president of Curtis Manufacturing Company, a producer of pneumatic machines. The original cost of his residence was $35,000. His family lived in the house until the 1970s.

This 1927 residence rises up in a crisp Tudor Revival style. Clean brickwork with bright cut stone trim and Gothic motifs are capped by a sweeping slate tile

The Walter Hecker House

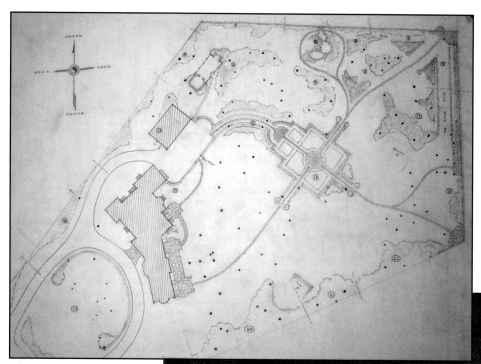

THE WALTER HECKER
HOUSE. ABOVE: SITE PLAN.
RIGHT: LIVING ROOM.
FACING PAGE, TOP: STAIR
HALL. FACING PAGE,
BOTTOM: DINING ROOM.

roof. An impressive carved stone entranceway is topped with a stone oriel above the double doors. Following the curve of the drive, the living room wing angles toward the street with a good view of the heavy timber-enclosed porch on the second floor with brick buttresses below. A fine one-and-a-half-story four-car garage sits toward the garden side of the house. Extensive gardens complete the grounds including a tool house and a decorative brick-walled, leaf-burning kiln.

Proceeding through the entry vestibule, a vaulted rotunda unites the living room, dining room, and a similarly proportioned stair hall rotunda beyond. Down five steps, the sunken living room's massive timber ceiling design appears slightly vaulted even though there is a full second floor above. This space features an intricately carved stone fireplace opposite a floor-to-ceiling leaded glass bay. At the far end of the room, a sunroom with a stone garden pool captures the southern light. The dining room, with walls covered in wood paneling and a decorative plaster ceiling above, is seen through wrought-iron gates. The vaulted breakfast room enjoys its own stone garden pool set within an east-facing bay. As in the S. Watts Smyth residence, there is a small radio room on the first floor near the entrance. Up on the second floor the master suite steps up above the living room with an adjoining sleeping porch. A study is situated off the stair hall over the main entrance. There are an additional three family bedrooms, three baths, and a second sleeping porch.

Located down the far end of the back stretch is the **John Latzer House**. This eclectic French Regency–style brick residence, built two years after the Hecker house, is curiously placed on its lot with the main entrance façade facing the side; the garden elevation is fully open to the street. Palladian details, French doors, wrought-iron balconies, two-story brick pilasters, and a Federal-style entry all work together to create a singular design. The main hall, with its grand proportions, is the second largest space in this residence. The hall leads directly into the dining room and breakfast room beyond. To one side, the living room with its five sets of French doors extends away from the main block of the house, creating an "L" in plan. On the opposite side of the main hall, the main stair rises to a Palladian window grouping at the landing. A study with built-in bookcases completes the first-floor public spaces. At the top of the main stair a sitting hall with its own fireplace connects the five family bedrooms and three baths. Tucked over the first-floor pantry and servants' dining room are two maids' rooms with bath.

John Latzer became president of Pet Milk Company in 1924 and served in that capacity until his death in 1952. During his tenure as president he built a

The John Latzer House

vast operation by acquiring numerous businesses relating to the dairy industry. He is said to have only missed three days of work during his fifty years of service with the company. Latzer received both bachelor's and master's degrees from the University of Illinois in Urbana. His father, Louis, an original developer of processing condensed milk, founded Helvetia Milk Condensing Company in Highland, Illinois, in 1885. The company changed the name to Pet Milk and moved its headquarters to St. Louis where it expanded to include twenty-two manufacturing plants at the time of Latzer's death. The family sold its Maritz & Young house following his death.

Continuing our track analogy, the third turn to the homestretch is filled with Maritz & Young houses, six in all. The three on the inside begin with the **Kenneth Davis House**. Davis was president of C. R. H. Davis Real Estate Company and the Federal Investment Company, both located at 4444 Olive Street. He and his wife, Virginia, had a son and daughter. Davis suffered from a nervous ailment for years before committing suicide in his bedroom in 1942.

Situated among the European traditional designs on Brentmoor is this Colonial-inspired residence. The symmetrical brick façade with stone keystones above the double-hung windows is capped by wooden dormers projecting above the slate roof. To the right of the residence is a three-car garage accessible through an open arched gallery positioned diagonally from the main house. A continuous wrought-iron balcony connects a series of five French doors on the second floor of the garden façade. The plan is a simple center hall layout with the living room stretching from front to rear. On each side of the centrally located fireplace are steps leading to the sunken sunroom. The second floor includes five bedrooms with oak floors and three baths. The original cost of this 1925 house was $42,000. The residence has since been torn down and replaced with a modern house.

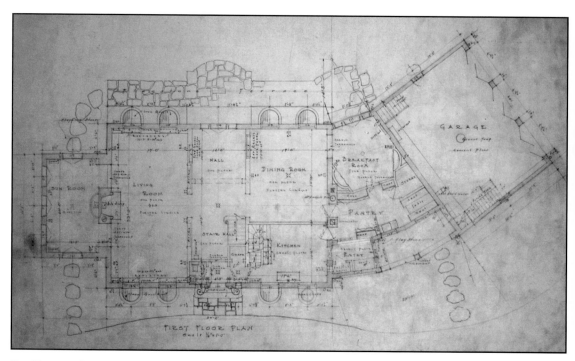

THE KENNETH DAVIS HOUSE, FIRST-FLOOR PLAN

THE ARCHITECTURE OF MARITZ & YOUNG

THE KENNETH DAVIS HOUSE, GARDEN VIEW (FRONT PICTURED ON PAGE 23)

Next door is the **John O'Fallon Jr. House**. Constructed in 1924, this stately brick Tudor Revival residence is dominated by the porte-cochere at the entrance. Three symmetrical gables identify the main block of the home with the service wing to the left in stucco, brick, and timber. Cut stone details including some stone finials at the roof create a formal air. Multiple brick and stone bays at the second floor add depth to the elevations. The garden (or rear) elevation reveals a center bay with decorative turned post details at the second-floor openings.

THE JOHN O'FALLON JR. HOUSE, LODGE ROOM

Visitors enter through arched, glazed steel doors into the central main hall with its beamed ceiling and stone-trimmed arches. The sunroom is directly ahead with a garden pool nestled within a bay. To the right, the living room extends the length of the hall. Wood-paneled walls, decorative plaster

ABOVE: THE JOHN
O'FALLON JR. HOUSE
FRONT. LEFT: SUNROOM.
FACING PAGE, TOP: ENTRY
HALL. FACING PAGE,
BOTTOM: LIVING ROOM.

ceiling, and carved stone fireplace combine to produce an English country flavor. The left side of the main hall opens to the formal dining room with a stone fireplace and the main stair to the second floor.

The second-floor layout similarly revolves around a central main hall including an elegantly detailed master suite with fireplace, a very generous sitting room also with its own fireplace, and two additional bedrooms and baths. Over the service wing there are two maids' rooms and bath, a sewing room, and a "man's room" and bath over the garage. In the basement, a fourteen-foot-high beamed ceiling is found in the lodge, with its fireplace, built-in bookcases, and large leaded casement window grouping trimmed in stone allowing abundant natural light into this dignified space.

John O'Fallon Jr. was a descendant of early St. Louis history. He shared the name of his great-grandfather, who made his fortune in military supplies, banking, railroads, and real estate, and was the nephew of explorer William Clark. The O'Fallon Jr. résumé consisted of a Yale education and service as a captain in World War I. He went on to establish O'Fallon Railroad Supply Company. In 1923, he married Harriot Evans and the couple moved into their Maritz & Young home the following year. O'Fallon was a member of both Bellerive and St. Louis country clubs.

Around the curve next to the O'Fallon residence is the **Louis Mahler House**. Constructed in 1923, this was the first Maritz & Young house in Brentmoor Park. The Wisconsin native was the president of Mahler Machine Supply Company. He was a mechanical engineer practicing in both the United States and Europe. According to Elizabeth Young's diaries, the Mahlers socialized with their architect and his wife. Louis Mahler had been retired for twenty-five years at the time of his death in 1948.

Approaching the residence, an airy, triple-arch loggia shelters the main entrance. Above the center arch, a stone oriel projects out from the second floor. Brick and stone accents are massed in pleasing proportions in this Tudor Revival with some stucco and half-timber elements utilized. Dormers and gable windows extend the elevation upward. To the left of the entrance, a distinctive two-story bay is capped by a crenellated parapet. The most forward projecting bay features a parapet with three carved stone finials. At the far right, a covered porch continues the open feeling of the front elevation. A detached four-car garage, which includes a bathroom, is situated to the garden side of the residence.

The main stairway rises up parallel to the small vaulted-gallery entrance. Beyond the stairs is the library, with its own exterior access. The living room, down two steps, has a symmetrical layout with a fireplace situated directly opposite a generous window bay. Beyond the living room, down two more steps is

THE LOUIS MAHLER HOUSE, FRONT ELEVATION

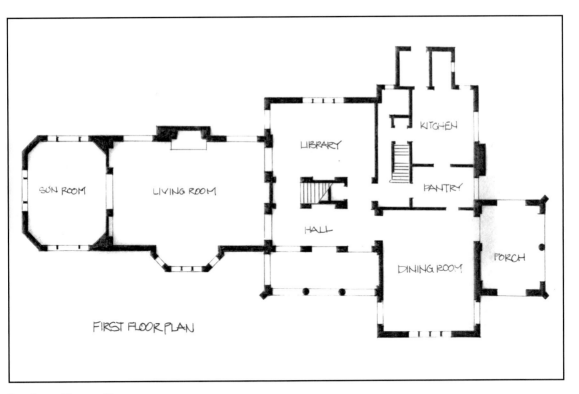

SUN ROOM

LIVING ROOM

LIBRARY

KITCHEN

PANTRY

HALL

DINING ROOM

PORCH

FIRST FLOOR PLAN

THE LOUIS MAHLER HOUSE, FIRST-FLOOR PLAN

a sunroom; the four corners of this room are angled to give the impression of an octagonal space. At the opposite end of the entrance gallery is the dining room. From this room, a pair of French doors leads out to a covered porch at the side of the residence. On the second floor there are four bedrooms, a sleeping porch, a den, and three baths. The third level provides for two servants' rooms and a bath.

Across the street from the Davis house is one of the largest and most expensive of the Maritz & Young houses, costing approximately $60,000 to build in 1927. The **William Moulton House** sits on a corner lot and has an oval driveway that leads through a porte-cochere between the house and the four-car, one-and-a-half-story detached garage. According to the 1930 census, besides their five children, the family had a butler, a cook, and a maid living on the premises. Moulton's son, also named William, lived in the house while he was president of the shoe company Moulton-Bartley, Inc.

William Moulton Sr., the fourth president of International Shoe Company, began his career in shoes at the age of fifteen in his hometown of Brookfield, Massachusetts. He worked for a Tennessee shoe manufacturer when he married Irene Watkins in 1900; Irene was the sister of Horton Watkins, another International Shoe executive. Moulton returned to New England to supervise the factory of W. H. McElwain Company before coming to St. Louis to work for Roberts, Johnson

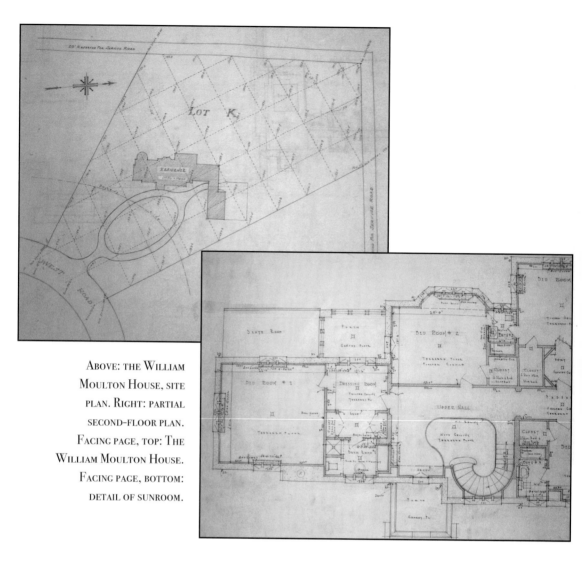

ABOVE: THE WILLIAM MOULTON HOUSE, SITE PLAN. RIGHT: PARTIAL SECOND-FLOOR PLAN. FACING PAGE, TOP: THE WILLIAM MOULTON HOUSE. FACING PAGE, BOTTOM: DETAIL OF SUNROOM.

& Rand Shoe Company, which a few years later merged to become International Shoe Company. By 1915, as a vice president, Moulton was responsible for all manufacturing. When he was named president in 1930, the company had thirty-nine factories and produced over 47 million pairs of shoes annually. He resigned the presidency in 1939 but continued as a director. A fellow director said of him in the *25th Anniversary Progress Club, International Shoe Company*, "He is perhaps the most widely known and one of the best liked men in the company, and in the industry." After Moulton's death, his wife had another house constructed in Brentmoor.

One could picture this mansion sitting atop a knoll in the rural English countryside. This stone Tudor Revival house extends 135 feet from bow to stern, with over 13,000 square feet of living space. The front elevation is made up of five gables and heavy stone lintels over the casement windows. The largest window,

located at the stairwell, rests under a segmented arch. Two massive triple chimneys rise above the multicolored slate roof.

Entering the house through a five-foot-wide, castle-like, solid-wood arched door brings a visitor to a vestibule and then into the main hall, featuring a grand curved staircase. Three arches lead to the sunroom with its bay window and door at the rear of the house. The living room is beautifully detailed with an ornamental plaster ceiling, wood-paneled walls, and terrazzo flooring. The right side of the first floor contains the kitchen, pantry, laundry, and servants' dining area. The second floor contains nine bedrooms (two over the garage), seven bathrooms, and two sleeping porches. The April 1930 issue of *Architectural Record* mentioned that the house had ten telephone outlets, including one in the garage and one in the servants' quarters.

Next door is the **Jerome Schotten House**. Schotten ran the family business, William Schotten Coffee Company, which was started as a grocery business by his grandfather in 1847. Jerome took over the presidency after his father died in a traffic accident in 1919. Schotten was born in 1882 in St. Louis and attended Saint Louis University. He was a member of Bellerive Country Club. He and his wife, Grace, lived in this house until the 1950s.

The residence is a non-fussy design in the Tudor Revival style. It was constructed in 1925, the same year as the Davis house across the street. The brickwork is judiciously accented with stone corbels and some window detailing. Brick gables include a raised diagonal (diaper) design. Timber lintels are located above most of the casement window groupings. The entrance side is anchored by the projecting center bay with almost equal wings to either side. Further to the right, the attached one-and-a-half-story garage helps to give the main house greater importance and height.

The plan is laid out in a cross pattern with the living room to the left, the stair hall and dining room in the center, and the kitchen, office, and service area to the right. The master bedroom with a fireplace, a sleeping porch above the dining room, and two additional bedrooms and baths are located on the second

THE JEROME SCHOTTEN HOUSE

THE ARCHITECTURE OF MARITZ & YOUNG

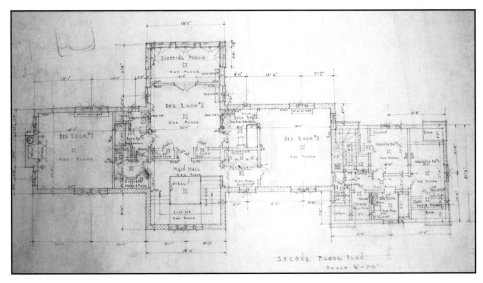

THE JEROME SCHOTTEN HOUSE, SECOND-FLOOR PLAN

floor. Above the garage are two servants' rooms and a bath. Two additions were planned after initial construction, adding a study and porch adjacent to both the living and dining rooms and a bay extending the dining room slightly beyond the sleeping porch above.

The final Maritz & Young residence in Brentmoor Park is the **Theodore Moreno House**. This is an impressive undertaking in a neoclassical interpretation. The brickwork is accented with cut stone including the four dramatic two-story columns at the main entrance. The overall massing (general shape and size) of the front elevation emphasizes a symmetry about its central pedimented bay, which affords visitors protection from the elements by the arched portico. The projecting wings to either side are subordinate. The garage pavilion is connected to the main residence by a porte-cochere.

THE THEODORE MORENO HOUSE, LIVING ROOM

The visitor enters a small vestibule through decorative wrought-iron gates into the main hall, the largest space in this residence. Ahead, through more wrought-iron work, is the dining room; an octagonal breakfast room lies adjacent. To the left is

Above: the Theodore Moreno House. Below: stair hall.

The Architecture of Maritz & Young

THE THEODORE MORENO HOUSE, BEDROOM

the living room and farther along, through three arches, is a brightly lit sunroom
with a fountain and stone garden pool. The dramatically open main stair rises up
to a broad landing highlighted by a Palladian window grouping and then splitting off to either side of the space, doubling back to a sweeping balcony above.
Wrought-iron railings wrap the terrazzo stairs and balcony to the second floor.

Theodore Moreno was a vice president at International Shoe Company working alongside his neighbor William Moulton. He lived with his wife, Florence, and
their daughter and at least six household staff. The Georgia native had worked
for the railroad before accepting a position with Roberts, Johnson & Rand Shoe
Company to manage its Hannibal, Missouri, factory. In 1913 he settled in St.
Louis as a vice president and director for International Shoe. He retired just
prior to Moulton taking over the presidency, though he remained on the board
until 1952.

Carrswold Drive

Carrswold Drive in Clayton is named for Robert Carr (1827–1901), who owned a large estate including the grounds of present-day Carrswold. He was a successful businessman connected to banking and railroads. The land was acquired from Carr's estate in 1922 by local businessmen, including later homeowners Oscar Buder, Harry Carson, and J. W. Leigh.

Carrswold consists of twenty-three houses on thirty-five tree-shaded acres. The undulating loop drive was designed by prominent Chicago landscape architect Jens Jensen in 1922. The Danish-born designer created Columbus Park in Chicago and several other parks around the Midwest. He designed landscapes for the estates of wealthy clients such as the Fords and Florsheims; his acquaintances included the likes of Frank Lloyd Wright, Jane Addams, and Carl Sandburg.

Jensen introduced green space, or common park grounds, for Carrswold and shielded the back or garden views of the houses in the middle of the loop by planting trees along the property lines where the terrain dropped steeply to the common ground area. Many of the houses sit high above the drive, as Jensen intended: "You want to go up to a house, not down to it."

The articles of agreement for Carrswold required houses to have at least two stories. The articles also stipulated that garage doors not be visible at the front of the house and the garages should be "the same style of architecture, structure and material as that of the dwelling so as to harmonize with it." Fences were also prohibited. Today, Carrswold is listed in the National Register of Historic Places.

Maritz & Young designed fourteen houses on Carrswold Drive (a fifteenth house is attributed to them, but no records or drawings have been found.) Their houses were constructed between 1925 and 1931.

Note: Like its neighbors in Brentmoor Park, Carrswold is a private drive and should not be toured.

On the inner circle of Carrswold, the first Maritz & Young residence is the **George Tom Murphy House**. Constructed in 1928 on a corner lot, this Tudor Revival design is sited toward the rear of the property with the garden view as the public face. The entrance drive approaches from the side, whereas the entrance front is concealed from the street. A stair tower block is capped with a hip roof under which a wide band of brickwork finishes off the rubble stonework below.

Above: the George Tom Murphy House. Below: garden view.

ABOVE: THE GEORGE TOM MURPHY HOUSE, LIVING ROOM. BELOW: DINING ROOM.

The stair tower hip roof continues through to the garden elevation. At the service wing a distinctive gabled dormer rises through the roof.

As one enters under the circular stair, the loggia opens to an exterior stone terrace. The wood-paneled living room is laid out symmetrically with a marble and wood detailed fireplace. At the end of the room, French doors lead to a covered porch and then to a stone terrace. The dining room—with classical themed murals covering the four walls in this nearly square space—is accessed through the loggia. On the second floor there are four bedrooms and two baths. A large enclosed sleeping porch above the service wing can be accessed through the second bedroom. With the garages in the basement and the parking court at the same level, an outdoor stone stairway leads up to the side entrance cleverly handled through a retaining wall and a covered porch adjacent to the main stair hall and entry.

George Tom Murphy was a real estate dealer. His family was among the founders of St. Louis County National Bank. Two doors down on Carrswold Drive lived Edith Schofield, sister of Murphy's wife, Vivian. The building permit for this house was initiated by Carrswold trustee Harry Carson, who apparently had the house built and sold it to Murphy. After Murphy's retirement, he and his wife traveled extensively throughout Europe and other areas of the world. He passed away at home following a lengthy illness.

Next door is the **Henry Brinckwirth House**. From the street a varied combination of rooflines creates interest in this grand Tudor Revival residence. Decorative gables of brick, stone, and half-timbering, along with a steep, slate hip roof over the stair tower, all contribute to the old world feel. The stone and brick

THE HENRY BRINCKWIRTH HOUSE, WATERCOLOR

Above: the Henry Brinckwirth
House. Left: Henry and Virginia
Brinckwirth in their living room.
Below: bedroom. Facing page, top:
the Brinckwirth House loggia.
Facing page, bottom: living room.

entrance bay greets visitors with its battered buttresses and carved stone details. An eighteen-foot-high window allows abundant light into the French-inspired stair tower. The driveway winds down to arched basement garage openings at the side elevation, where all four levels of this residence are revealed. A distinctive feature of note on the garden side is a second-floor recessed gallery supported by turned wood posts and a projecting wrought-iron balcony.

Henry Brinckwirth was a descendant of a pioneering brewing family. His grandfather Theodore founded Lafayette Brewery in 1848. The brewery later changed its name to Brinckwirth-Nolker Brewing Company when Henry's father,

Louis, co-managed the company with his mother and brother-in-law. Henry and his brother and sister were raised by their uncles, John Grone and Henry Griesedieck Jr., following the deaths of their parents in 1911. Henry married Virginia Wagner in 1928 and had their Carrswold house built two years later. They were inspired by Tudor-style architecture after honeymooning in England.

The vaulted main hall with its circular stairs leads into the vaulted loggia through a series of three arched openings. The large oak-paneled living room with its decorative plaster ceiling lies to the left with access to both the loggia and main entrance hall. At either side of the fireplace, French doors lead to a generous outdoor covered porch supported by stone arches. There is an easy flow moving from the living room, through the loggia, into the dining room with its beamed ceiling, and into the small, vaulted breakfast room. A library is tucked away through a compact vaulted gallery; built-in bookcases and a stone fireplace complete this private space.

Four of the five family bedrooms open off the second-floor sitting hall, where the covered gallery and balcony overlook the garden. A comfortable covered sleeping porch can be accessed through the master bedroom. Three maids' rooms and a bath can be found over the service wing. A billiards room with a fireplace and beamed ceiling occupies a portion of the basement along with the garage, laundry, and a man's bedroom and bath.

Continuing up the drive one sees the **Edith Schofield House**. The building permit for this house was also initiated by trustee Harry Carson, who apparently had the house built and sold it to Schofield in 1928. Edith Dulany Schofield came from a family of lumber company owners in Hannibal. In 1931 she married Homer Klein, vice president of Cupples Company. James Maritz, Raymond's brother, purchased the house in the mid-1940s.

The house is in the Tudor Revival style with typical exterior materials of stone, patterned brick, stucco, and wood siding. The robust front façade, topped with a red clay tile roof, consists of a central entrance bay with a recessed gallery at the first floor. An exterior covered passageway connects the attached garage to the kitchen and main entrance hall. A balanced composition is achieved with the four gables and a chimney rendered in stone and brick. The rear façade contains the centrally located dining room bay with a projecting timber bay at the second floor. A series of French doors serve as exterior access for both the living and dining rooms. The floor plan is simple in concept, revolving around the gracious central stair hall. On the second floor, four bedrooms and two baths serve the owners, with two servants' rooms and a bath over the three-car garage.

The Edith Schofield House, front (above) and garden view (below)

The third house associated with Carson is aptly named the **Harry Carson House**. Harry Carson was president of the St. Louis Stock Exchange and a Carrswold trustee. He obtained the permit for this house and began construction. Unfortunately, during construction in 1929 the stock market crashed, followed by Carson's death that December. The house was left empty for nearly a decade until it was purchased by Harry O'Neil, a district manager for F. W. Woolworth Company.

This is a Tudor Revival residence with a strong French influence in stone and slate. An unassuming entrance with brick quoins set within the stone façade stands beneath a delicate wrought-iron balcony supported upon stone brackets. Steep hip roofs replace the usual gable ends on the street façade, contributing to the relatively modest scaling of the home. The overall plan is in an L-shape with bays stepping toward the street. A distinctive feature of the front elevation is the octagonal stair tower with its pointed roof. Stone garden walls extending from

THE HARRY CARSON HOUSE, FRONT ELEVATION

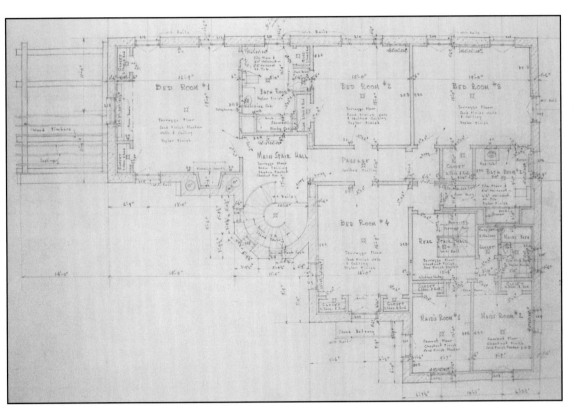

THE HARRY CARSON HOUSE, SECOND-FLOOR PLAN

either side of the house delineate the public side from the garden side. French doors dominate the garden elevation with wrought-iron railings at a majority of the openings.

The residence is entered through a deep recessed porch. The entrance hall opens directly ahead to the loggia from which two pairs of arched-top French doors lead outdoors to stone steps down to an enclosed grassy terrace. Access to the living room is through the circular main stair hall and down six steps. A wood-beamed ceiling in this room continues through to the loggia, which overlooks the sunken living room. An outdoor pergola lies immediately off the living room at the terrace level. On the second floor, there are four family bedrooms and two baths with an additional two maids' rooms and a bath. The three-car garage is situated in the basement.

The final Maritz & Young residence on the inner circle is the **W. Palmer Clarkson House**. Brick, cut stone accents, and a slate tile roof are familiar materials in another Tudor Revival design, this one constructed in 1931. Curiously, the garden elevation, with its wrought-iron railings and panel supports, is evocative of New Orleans.

The W. Palmer Clarkson House, front elevation (above) and door detail (left). Inset: Clarkson.

William Palmer Clarkson (1867–1940) joined Pioneer Cooperage Company in 1902 and within twenty years became president. The company operated factories in St. Louis and Chicago and plants in the South. Pioneer was the largest producer of barrels in the world and owned a large amount of timber acreage in the southern United States. Clarkson first came to St. Louis with his family when he was seven. He received a law degree from Washington University and joined a St. Louis law firm before starting his own practice. Clarkson served as president or director of countless organizations including the board of education and Bellefontaine Cemetery, where his body now rests. In 1897, he married

Marie Turner, whose mother, Blanche Soulard, was a descendant of one of the oldest families in St. Louis.

As one enters the house through an enclosed vestibule, the light-filled stairs lie ahead in the main stair hall, splitting to either side at the landing and doubling back to the second floor. The flooring is in a diamond design in terrazzo. Very conducive to entertaining, the living room and wood-paneled library lie to the right, and the dining room is through a thirty-four-inch-deep arch to the left of the stair hall, all on the same level. The library floor is unusual, with wood parquet set within a terrazzo border. An outdoor covered porch is accessed through a door from the library, which in turn is adjoined by an open terrace accessed through the dining room. The elevated terrace leads down to a further terrace by way of two stone curved stairs. On the second floor, the sitting area at the top of the stairs features a fireplace and vaulted ceiling above. There are three comfortable bedrooms each with an individual bath. One bedroom has access to an open porch deck.

Among the Maritz & Young residences on the outer loop of Carrswold Drive is the **Richard Waltke House**. Louis Waltke, Richard's father, was president of William Waltke & Company, a soap manufacturer established by his father. The 1930 census lists Richard as an officer (secretary) at an investment company he managed with his two brothers. He and his wife, Florence, had three children. Waltke was a member of both the Missouri Athletic Club and Sunset Hill Country Club (now Sunset Country Club in Sunset Hills). He sold the Carrswold house in 1934.

The stately two-story brick Tudor Revival residence has a typical slate roof and restrained stone details evident in the exterior design. An entrance porch with crenellated brickwork and stonework indicates a deep vestibule. To the left, an arcade protects an exterior passage from the garage to a side entrance. Further to the right of the entry, past the stair tower, a glazed double archway encloses the west wall of the loggia, creating balance. The cost of construction was $32,000.

On the entrance façade, the large chimney massing cleverly disguises the fact that the living room fireplace is actually located to the right of the vertical chimney stacks, centered between the two first-floor casement windows. This is achieved by running the interior flue at a forty-five-degree angle between the fireplace and the exterior vertical stacks.

As one enters the covered vestibule into a compact entrance hall, the large main stair hall is to the right with a generous circular stair. Continuing through to the loggia, the sunken living room lies beyond. The main dining room, with an

The Richard Waltke House, front (top) and front elevation (below). Facing page: garden view (top). Lower left: bathroom. Lower right: stair hall.

adjoining breakfast room, is also accessed through the loggia. An attached three-bay garage is entered from the side. Including staff quarters, this residence has eight bedrooms and six baths on the second floor.

Richard Waltke had a second Maritz & Young house constructed in Ladue. Although that house is also in Tudor style, the exterior utilizes stone and half-timber work instead of the brick used on the Carrswold house. Both residences have equally grand spiral stairs.

THE SECOND RICHARD WALTKE
HOUSE IN LADUE (ABOVE) AND ITS
STAIR HALL (RIGHT)

Next door to the Waltke residence in Clayton is the **Albert Keller House**. This sophisticated, French-influenced design in cut limestone was constructed in 1929. Carved stone keystones, dormer fronts, and stone columns indicate a high attention to detail. Below the slate-clad hip roofs, decorative conductor heads connect the gutters to the downspouts. Glazed wrought-iron vestibule doors, set within a carved stone frame and flanked by oval niches, feature prominently beneath a splendid iron and glass porte-cochere at the main entrance. As with many Maritz & Young residences, the walled parking court is entered below decorative wrought-iron overwork supporting a lantern.

Albert Keller married Nellie Brown, the youngest daughter of Paul Brown, who made a fortune in tobacco before starting an investment firm in his own name. Keller was involved with Paul Brown & Company and the Mercantile Trust Company, both established by his father-in-law. He served as chairman of Barnes Hospital and president of Municipal Theater Association. Born in Lexington,

The Albert Keller House

The Albert Keller House, garden view (above) and first-floor plan

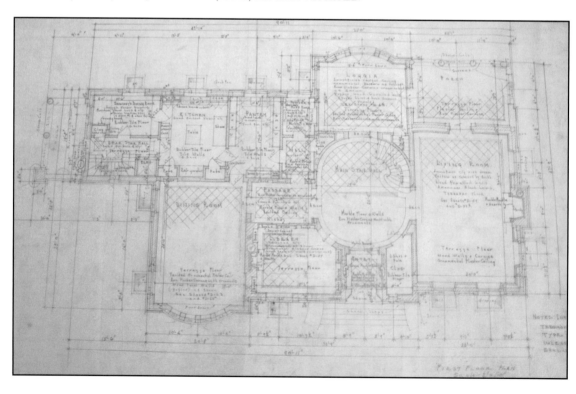

Missouri, Keller operated a department store in Marshall, Missouri, before heading to St. Louis to work for Brown. He enjoyed collecting rare books and first editions, which he kept in a library lined with bookshelves. Keller also spent time at his 1,000-acre farm in Callaway County. Nellie outlived her husband by eleven years and remained in the house until her death in 1967.

Visitors stepping into the large, oval main stair hall must have felt like they were entering a symphony hall with marble covering the floor and walls. Four arches lead off the main hall to the library, loggia, living room, and vaulted ceiling passageway to the dining room. In addition to the servants' dining room on the first floor, there are two maids' rooms on the second floor along with three bedrooms for the family, including the master suite containing a large dressing room behind sliding doors.

The **Oscar Buder House** is located on a rear corner lot. This was the first Maritz & Young house built on Carrswold. Oscar Buder was an original trustee of the Carrswold neighborhood. His family was in the newspaper business, owning both the *St. Louis Times* and the *Westliche Post* in St. Louis. Buder, who was trained as a lawyer at Washington University, was a junior partner at Buder & Buder located in, appropriately, the Buder Building. Among his civic duties, he

THE OSCAR BUDER HOUSE

THE OSCAR BUDER HOUSE, PLAY-
GROUND (ABOVE) AND STAIR HALL

served on the election commit-
tee for the City of St. Louis. His
son, Eugene, was a prominent
local attorney. Buder Park and
other educational institutions
in St. Louis are named for the
family.

The residence is a French
Eclectic design in brick, stucco, and inset brickwork. In
plan, the living room wing and
garage wing are sited at oblique
angles to the main center block. The tile roof is steeply pitched over the varied
blocks, yielding a charming composition. A private formal French entrance bay
is found on the rear side of the residence as the garden side is facing the street.
A fine wrought-iron balcony extends over the entry doors. Adding to the eclectic
design is the combination of double-hung and casement windows appearing on
the garden side.

The sunroom lies directly ahead from the two-story stair hall with a patterned terrazzo floor. To the right, at an angle, is the living room. At the far end of the room, French doors open onto an L-shaped covered porch. Beyond the kitchen, a two-car garage and servants' porch occupy a story-and-a-half wing on angle to the main house. Four bedrooms on the second floor share two baths. A sleeping porch, off the master bedroom and above the covered porch below, is framed in heavy timber. Several outbuildings include a children's playhouse.

Ella Peters Lauman was surrounded by shoes her entire life. Her father, Henry Peters, established Peters Shoe Company and was instrumental in the creation of International Shoe Company in 1911. Her two brothers, Edwin and Oliver, were both executives with International Shoe. Oliver and Ella lived together in the **Peters-Lauman House**. Ella's husband, Arthur Lauman, died in 1918 before the Maritz & Young house was built. Ella outlived him by fifty-three years. When Ella died in 1971 (Oliver had passed away one year earlier), the estate was donated to Barnes and St. Luke's hospitals.

Similar to the Oscar Buder House, the positioning of the 1930 residence is unusual in that the entrance elevation actually faces the rear of the lot. The entry

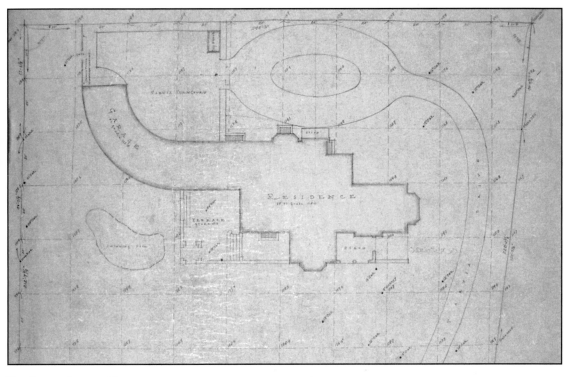

THE PETERS-LAUMAN HOUSE, SITE PLAN

The Peters-Lauman House, FRONT ELEVATION (ABOVE) AND GARDEN VIEW

and parking court are both hidden from public view. This Tudor Revival in stone and slate has a connected garage structure laid out on a curve with four car bays with a man's room and bath above. The main entry to the residence is through a Gothic stone arch leading to a covered porch. From the street, an impressive projecting bay rises up from the basement level.

Inside the house, the main circular stair sweeps above the entry. Beyond the stair hall, another vaulted rotunda leads to the living room, sunroom, and dining room. In the basement, a billiards room curiously leads to separate men's and women's locker rooms with showers and outdoor access for future swimming pool access.

Built a year before the Peters-Lauman House, the **James Harris House** was the residence for the president of Harris-Polk Hat Company. After his death, his wife, Maude, continued to live in the house until selling it in the 1950s. The couple had two daughters.

This New England Colonial–style design has the feeling of a home that has been added to over time. The two-story brick main house is flanked on either side by one-and-a-half-story wings; the service wing includes a three-car garage, and the opposite wing consists of a sunken living room. Brick dentils (projecting blocks) are featured just below the second-floor levels. Double-hung windows dominate the elevations with arched casements roofed in copper above the slate tile roof. The Palladian-style entrance is highlighted by a painted wood pediment extending over the sidelights and door. A covered porch supported by heavy timbers extends from the living room elevation. Upstairs are seven bedrooms and four baths.

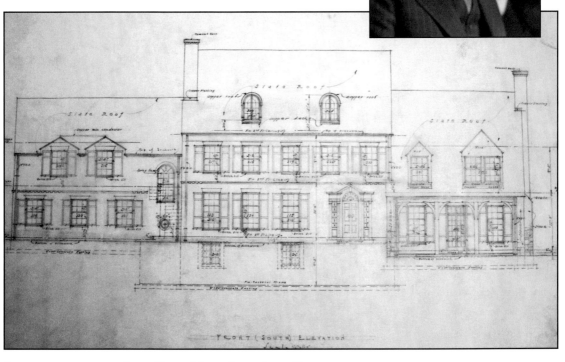

FRONT ELEVATION OF THE JAMES HARRIS HOUSE. INSET: JAMES HARRIS.

Around the curve in the drive are two houses for the same family: the **David Woods House** and the Robert Arthur House. David Woods's name appears on the drawings for both houses. Woods, another International Shoe Company employee, retired in 1928. He had worked for a Memphis railroad where he met Theodore Moreno, who later helped him enter the shoe business. Woods came to St. Louis in 1906 and spent over twenty years with the shoe company working in both accounting and auditing. He was responsible for introducing improvements in accounting methods companywide. He was named a director of International Shoe in 1914. Woods and his wife, Martha, were born in Kentucky. Mary, one of their three daughters, and son-in-law Robert Arthur lived in the house until their own Maritz & Young house was completed next door.

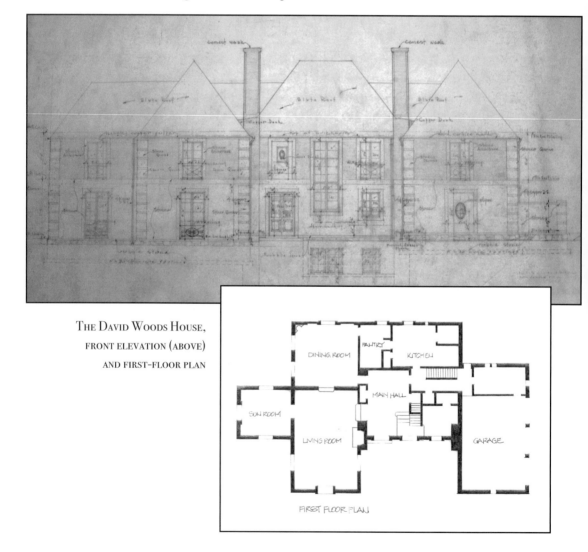

THE DAVID WOODS HOUSE,
FRONT ELEVATION (ABOVE)
AND FIRST-FLOOR PLAN

The Woods residence is an adaptation of an elegant eighteenth-century French structure with a classic center pavilion and projecting symmetrical wings rendered in brick and stucco. The steep, hip, slate-covered roof accentuates the French influence along with stucco quoins and trim surrounding the window and door openings. French doors abound beginning with the main entrance. At the rear elevation above the roof, a copper light monitor allows daylight into the back stair.

The main hall extends up to the second floor with terrazzo stairs rising to the right side. The living room and dining room are to the left, accessed through deep recesses. An enclosed sun porch projects out from the sunken living room with three sets of French doors opening to the exterior. Wood molding and wainscoting continue the French theme throughout the first-floor formal spaces. A side entrance three-car garage with a man's room and bath are integrated into the first-floor plan. The second floor has a small sitting room, four bathrooms, and six bedrooms, including a fireplace within the master bedroom.

David Woods had the house next door constructed for his daughter Mary and her husband in 1937. By this time, the firm was called Maritz, Young & Dusard after Rime Dusard joined it in 1934. Robert Arthur served as an officer with the Mississippi Valley Trust Company. He was retired as the bank vice president at the time of his death in 1983.

The **Robert Arthur House** was the final residence designed by Maritz, Young & Dusard on Carrswold Drive. Similar to the Woods house, this is another in a variation on the French provincial theme. Painted brickwork is used throughout the exterior with dentil trim accents and cornice work. A bow window highlights the first floor of the two-story main pavilion. At the second floor, pediments projecting above the cornice line give prominence to the windows. Note at the entrance that this section of the house is two full stories; however, at the garden elevation the roof carries downward to yield a one-and-a-half-story elevation. One-story hip-roof wings lie to either side of the main block, including a detached garage connected to the main house by a breezeway.

MARY ARTHUR, 1928

THE ROBERT ARTHUR HOUSE, FRONT (ABOVE) AND GARDEN VIEW (BELOW)

Two doors down is the **Lewis Jackson House**. Like Maritz & Young home-owners Oliver Peters, David Woods, Theodore Moreno, and William Moulton, Jackson was associated with the International Shoe Company. The Boston native came to St. Louis in 1923. He sold the house after his wife, Margaretta, died in 1941.

Constructed in 1929, the Jackson residence is a more modestly scaled Tudor Revival structure. Except for some half-timber and stucco work, various decora-

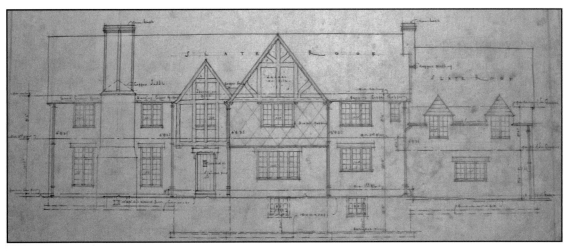

THE LEWIS JACKSON HOUSE, FRONT ELEVATION (ABOVE) AND SECOND-FLOOR PLAN (BELOW)

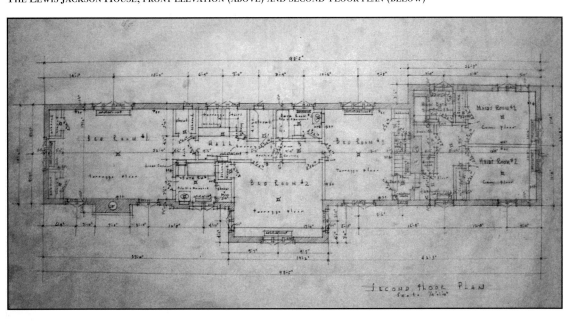

tive brickwork patterns predominate on the elevations. Heavy timber lintels are featured over first-floor casement window openings. This plan is linear in design; the house is only one room wide with the central dining room bay projecting to the front. An attached two-car garage is delineated by the lowering of its roof to break up the overall elevation. The first floor consists of the living room, a modest stair hall, the dining room, and the kitchen with a small dining alcove. On the second floor, three family bedrooms and two baths are balanced by two servants' rooms and bath over the garage.

The last Maritz & Young residence on Carrswold is the **Henry Whiteside House.** The residence is French in style with its elegant symmetrical façade

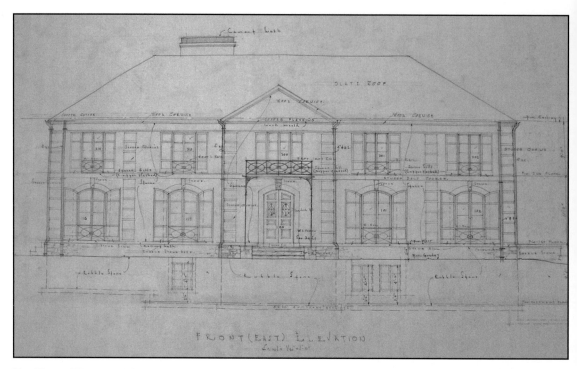

The Henry Whiteside House, front elevation (above) and side elevations (below)

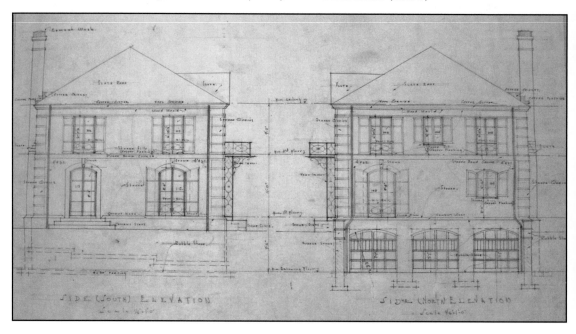

and multiple, segmented, arched French door openings. Except for the stone keystones above the first-floor arches and stone sill band, the exterior consists of stucco, including the decorative quoins. A slightly projecting central entrance bay is capped with a gabled pediment. The double-door entry is protected by a decorative wrought-iron porch and railing. Wrought-iron railings are featured at both the first-floor and second-floor window openings.

As one enters, the circular stairs climb to the second story from the diamond terrazzo stair hall floor. Painted wood trim, panel molding, and wainscoting carry into the living room, extending the entire depth of the house. A marble fireplace anchors the end wall of the room. Beyond the living room, a sunroom with similar flooring to the stair hall is entered through an arched opening. A covered porch connects to both the living room and sunroom through pairs of French doors. The dining room, breakfast room, kitchen, and pantry lie opposite the stair hall. On the second floor, there are three family bedrooms, a guest bedroom, and two baths, along with servants' quarters.

The homeowner, Henry Whiteside (1874–1937), was yet another man with connections to International Shoe Company. He worked for the shoe company called Roberts, Johnson & Rand that merged with other shoe companies in 1911 to become International Shoe. He sold his Carrswold house shortly before his death.

A Glimpse: International Shoe Company

Six owners of Maritz & Young houses in Brentmoor and Carrswold were associated with International Shoe Company, with countless other executives living around the area, including fashionable Portland Place. From the beginning, the company's mission was to produce quality shoes for the average person—in other words, to manufacture a great product to sell at low and medium prices.

St. Louis and shoes were together for much of the twentieth century. Numerous shoe companies have called St. Louis "home," including Hamilton-Brown, Peters, Wohl, Edison Brothers, Brown, and Roberts, Johnson & Rand.

International Shoe Company was established in 1911 when two St. Louis shoe companies joined forces, the Roberts, Johnson & Rand Shoe Company and the Peters Shoe Company. Jackson Johnson, who was the president of Roberts, Johnson & Rand, became the first president of the consolidated firm. He served

THE INTERNATIONAL
SHOE COMPANY
HEADQUARTERS ON
WASHINGTON AVENUE,
ST. LOUIS, CA. 1930

until 1915, at which time his brother Oscar took over. When Oscar died unexpectedly a year later, their first cousin Frank Rand became the third president of the company. His fourteen-year reign brought extraordinary growth to the company, especially during World War I when the War Department placed large orders for military footwear.

In 1921, International Shoe owned thirty-two factories in Missouri, Illinois, and Kentucky when they acquired W. H. McElwain Company, the same Boston shoe company that William Moulton had worked for before coming to St. Louis. Much as Maritz & Young prospered during the 1920s, International Shoe also increased profits and productivity. They were manufacturing over 54 million shoes annually by the end of the decade, a number that ranked them as the largest producer in the world.

Although the Depression years hurt the company, requiring layoffs and reduced wages, they survived better than most businesses owing to top-quality management including Maritz & Young homeowner William Moulton. Moulton stepped down as president at the end of the 1930s and was replaced by Byron Gray, another former employee of Roberts, Johnson & Rand.

The company's profits exploded during World War II, much as it did during the First World War, thanks to large government contracts. Employing 32,000 people in sixty-seven factories, International Shoe produced 33 million pairs of shoes for the government by the end of the war. They were the largest supplier in the nation of combat boots, submarine sandals, and paratrooper shoes.

Frank Rand, a founding member of the company, was still chairman of the board when he died in 1949. His sons Edgar and Henry took over running the company in successive terms, during which time they purchased the prominent Florsheim Shoe Company among their many acquisitions. They also formed a new division called International Retail Sales to expand their retail operations. When Maurice Chambers accepted the presidency in 1962, he expanded the business overseas and made acquisitions outside the shoe industry. A few years later the company decided to change its name to Interco to better fit its expanding business operations.

Forsyth Boulevard

Robert Forsyth was a gentleman farmer and land dealer born in 1808. Those who knew him described him as kind and generous. He was one of the largest land-owners in and around the current area of Forest Park along with Thomas Skinker, Isabella de Mun, Charles P. Chouteau, and his sister Julia Maffitt.

The Forsyth property was divided among his children when he died in 1873. The eastern portion was sold to the City of St. Louis to become part of Forest Park. Robert Forsyth's farmhouse became the Cottage Restaurant in the park, which operated until 1904. The western part of the property was purchased by Washington University for its campus.

ROBERT FORSYTH

Robert's daughter Laura and her husband, Edward Tesson, inherited the property on the south side of current-day Forsyth Boulevard, where the Maritz & Young houses are located. This area was leased to the Louisiana Purchase Exposition Company for the 1904 World's Fair. The land became the site of the Palace of Forestry, Fish and Game, and the French Pavilion, where young Raymond Maritz first became inspired to study architecture. The Wydown-Forsyth Historic District is listed in the National Register of Historic Places. Many of the nearly two hundred residences in the historic district were constructed between 1909 and 1941. Maritz & Young designed more than thirty houses there, including eight along Forsyth Boulevard.

—⁂—

Strolling the sidewalk on Forsyth Boulevard opposite Washington University, heading east toward Skinker Boulevard and the entrance to Forest Park, the first Maritz & Young residence one sees is the **Henry Friedman House**. Detroit native Henry Friedman graduated from the University of Michigan and studied at Harvard Law School. He then began working with his brother and Hungarian-born father, Nathan, founder of N. Friedman & Sons, established in 1875 as a manufacturer of ladies' apparel. The business later moved to St. Louis. Friedman loved to play golf and was a member of Westwood Country Club, another Maritz & Young project. He died in retirement in 1957.

THE HENRY FRIEDMAN HOUSE

The Friedman residence was constructed in 1927 in a Tudor Revival style. A colorful tile roof caps this rather sturdy-looking structure. Featured on the street elevation are a copper-roofed oriel or bay window feature, a massive double chimney rendered in brick with punched window openings at both the first and second floors, and a welcoming covered entrance porch with decorative wooden spindles. A brick, diamond-shaped or crisscross pattern (diaper) fills the gables around the house. Leaded casement windows are featured throughout with a half-timber rectangular bay projecting from the main structure.

The focal point in the spacious wood-paneled living room is the Gothic arched fireplace with French doors at either side. Contrasting with the living room, the dining room has an arched niche bay; the plaster molding around the room is elegant in its restraint. At the top of the curved stairs, a sitting room with a fireplace leads to two bedrooms and one bath with two maids' rooms and a bath. For summer comfort, a large sleeping porch is entered through one of the bedrooms. A two-car garage is incorporated into the first floor with a man's room located in the basement.

The Henry Friedman House, living room (above),
dressing room (left), and dining room (below)

Three houses down from the Friedman residence is the **L. Guy Blackmer House**. Blackmer (1881–1961) worked for the family business of manufacturing clay pipe and tile. Lucian Richmond Blackmer had established Blackmer & Post Pipe Company at the time his son was born in 1881. Guy Blackmer ran the business with his three brothers after the passing of their father. Guy was an expert in Chinese art and served on the board of the Saint Louis Art Museum for twenty-five years. He sold the Forsyth house in the early 1930s and was living on Kingsbury Avenue at the time of his death. His family also had a summer house named "Matoaka" in Maine.

Constructed in 1925, the Blackmer residence is also a Tudor Revival design yielding to some Norman influence with its small overhanging cornices. The simple, less formal design is both clean and elegant in appearance. Heavy timber lintels span the first floor, from the bank of leaded glass windows to the

BELOW: THE L. GUY BLACKMER HOUSE. INSET: L. GUY BLACKMER

The L. Guy Blackmer House, stair hall (above) and living room (below)

The Architecture of Maritz & Young

main entrance and the garage doors. An arched fan window above French doors is located at the interior stair landing, giving an asymmetrical but balanced look to this street view. The garage is located beyond the slate-covered parking court gate. As with a number of other Maritz & Young roof designs, the ridges turn upward toward the ends to lend an air of age and charm to the overall structure.

Rough plaster walls predominate throughout the inside of the house. The entry stair in wood leads up and over the front door. Flagstone covers most of the first floor. Both the living and dining rooms have wood-beamed ceilings and projecting bays to the south allowing plenty of light into the spaces.

Next door is the **William Lewin House**. Not to be outdone by his neighbors Friedman and Blackmer, William Lewin also worked and later became president of the family business, Lewin Metals Corporation. The company later merged with others and is now part of Cerro Flow Products. Lewin was born in Colorado in 1883 and served in the military during World War I. He and his wife, Mary, had two sons and a daughter. The residence is now owned by Washington University.

The William Lewin House

The William Lewin House, garden view (above) and
breakfast room (right)

This residence is a fine example of Spanish adaptation constructed in 1925. The book *Modern Homes: Their Design and Construction* (1930) described the house: "The walls of stucco and tile roof in variegated colors are typically Spanish, and the brick insets in the entrance archway, the capping of the service gate posts with brick and the shuttered windows are interesting details introduced into this house detail." A variety of pierced openings in the exterior walls and chimney along with a wrought-iron balcony reinforcing the importance of the main entrance provide interesting focal points along the street façade of the house. The predominant feature on the west elevation is the two-story living room wing with arched windows. A curious half-timber sleeping porch on the rear side extends off the master bedroom on the second floor. A double garage has been incorporated into the overall structure with arched doors all located beyond the impressive wooden service gates set in stucco walls.

The two-story-high stenciled timber ceiling is noteworthy above the sunken living room. One end of the living room opens to the hall and tiled circular stairs leading to a second-floor bridge that connects the three family bedrooms. Another interesting feature is the arched opening leading into the barrel-vaulted breakfast room. The room has a handsome arched door and sidelight combination, and the tiles on the floor are brought up the walls as a wainscot.

The next house, the third Maritz & Young residence in a row, is the **George Taylor House**. This residence, along with the William Moulton House in Brentmoor Park and the Frank Mayfield House in Ladue, is one of the largest from the Maritz & Young portfolio. The most imposing element of this

THE WILLIAM LEWIN HOUSE, LIVING ROOM

1925 Tudor Revival structure is the monumental circular stone and brick stair tower of Norman influence. The overall composition is well detailed in brick, cut stone, rough stone, heavy timber and stucco, and rustic slate roofing. The majority of leaded glass and steel sash windows have been set within cut stone framing, lending an air of refinement. A fine bay window detailed in cut stone and brick is positioned at the second-floor study, helping to offset the dominance of the stair tower along with the bold heavy timberwork over the main entrance. A semi-detached garage is located to the western end of the house connecting through a porte-cochere, further elongating the street elevation. The rear or garden side of the residence is a handsome arrangement of components similar to the street façade but with a more inviting presence. The central focus is the two-story bay at the dining room that opens up to the outside gardens and southern exposure. The rear yard originally included a circular lily pond centered by a sculpture.

George Taylor, the man who commissioned the house, was born in West Virginia and came to St. Louis in his twenties for employment with the Singer Sewing Machine Company. Taylor moved on to the insurance business by becoming

The George Taylor House,
front (above) and stair
hall (right)

a representative agent for New York Life Insurance and over the years became one of the highest producing salesmen for the company. He worked for the company up until his death in the mansion in 1935. His wife, Ida, was the sister of James Howe, founder of TUMS.

Inside, the entry hall leads into a spacious paneled reception hall. The most spectacular feature of the mansion is the castlelike stair tower with its rough stone walls, cantilevered circular stairs, and the heavy timber trusses framing the conical roof above. Details include the romantic wrought-iron railings with candle stands progressing up the stairs and a large custom chandelier

The George Taylor House, garden view (above) and dining room (left)

suspended from above. The well-proportioned living room opens up with its generous fireplace wrought in carved stone, a terrazzo floor, and a decorative plaster ceiling. A south-facing bay brings an abundance of light into the formal dining room. Upstairs, beyond two master bedrooms and two family bedrooms, are two servants' rooms, a study with a fireplace, and a cozy library also with its own fireplace. Today the house is owned by Washington University and used as the Catholic Student Center. A modern chapel has been added at the rear of the house.

Two doors down is the **Leroy Bush House**. This Tudor Revival house, constructed in 1923, greets visitors with a projecting, arched, stone entrance vesti-

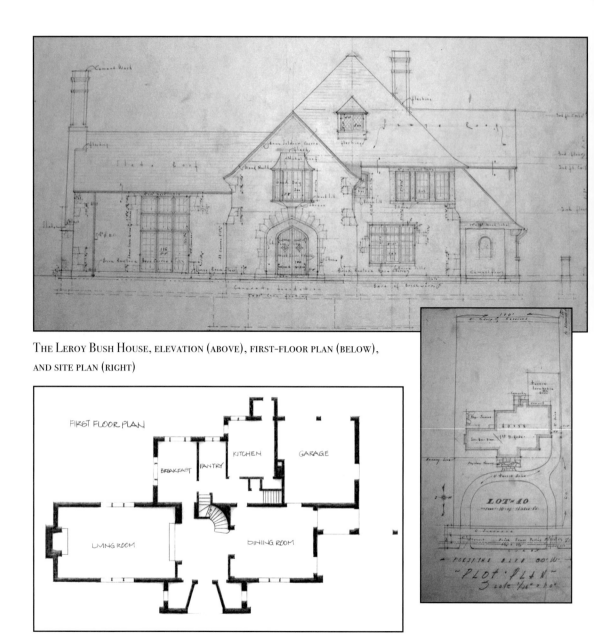

THE LEROY BUSH HOUSE, ELEVATION (ABOVE), FIRST-FLOOR PLAN (BELOW),
AND SITE PLAN (RIGHT)

bule with glass and wrought-iron doors. Exterior construction consists of brick with cut stone corbels and corner accents throughout. A slate tile roof typifies many homes of this time period with the roof slightly curving upward while approaching the eaves. Triple window combinations appear on the street façade, with the living room windows dominating in size and number.

The sunken vaulted living room with its terrazzo floor and dramatic stone fireplace is the highlight of this residence. This room enjoys light streaming in from both the front and back windows, giving the space an airy feeling with its twenty-foot-high vaulted ceiling. At one end of the living room, a balcony on the second floor opens up through an arch with a distinctive decorative timber column supporting the roof structure above. A circular staircase leads to the second floor containing three family bedrooms and two baths along with a maids' room and bath.

Leroy Bush was born in Mexico, Missouri, to Walter and Laura Bush. He was the president and treasurer of his family business, Romann & Bush Pig Iron & Coke Company, with offices in the Ambassador Building. Bush served his country as a first lieutenant in World War I. He and his wife, Florence, and their daughter moved from the house in the late 1920s. Bush died just a few years later at forty-six years of age. Florence took over the title of company president after her husband's death.

Another two houses down is the **Vincent Price House**. Vincent Leonard Price was born in Illinois. In 1894 he married Marguerite Willcox, and they raised four children, including Vincent Jr., the film actor. The elder Price's father, Vincent Clarence Price, was a chemist who invented baking powder and made his fortune manufacturing Dr. Price's Cream Baking Powder and later created the first fruit and herb flavoring extracts. His son, who had the Maritz & Young house commissioned, graduated from Yale and worked for his father at the Pan Confection Company in Chicago. He came to St. Louis after merging his father's confection company with two other candy manufacturers to establish the National Candy Company. The company's candy products had tremendous sales during the 1904 St. Louis World's Fair. The family lived on Washington Avenue before moving to a larger house on the same street. He later established Clinton Industries to manufacture corn syrup and starch. Price was actively involved with numerous organizations including the YMCA and the Boy Scouts. He retired in 1945 due to a painful arthritic condition, and when his wife suddenly passed away the following year, he sold the Forsyth house before moving to Tucson, Arizona, where he died in 1948.

Vincent Price Sr.

This residence, constructed in 1923, is a classic Georgian Revival design characterized by a clear sense of balance around a central axis. In *Vincent Price:*

THE VINCENT PRICE HOUSE

A Daughter's Biography, Victoria Price recalls her father's words about the house where he grew up: "The house was to be American, no question about that. The architects, a pair of nice young American men, were very much in vogue, naturally, since my parents had waited all these years and were going to have the best. . . . These two young men, I'm sure, matured rapidly as men and as architects after endless losing rounds with Mother." The actor said his parents wanted a classic New England–style house. "The two maturing architects were happy in this exterior triumph, but, unluckily for them, then wanted to carry it on inside."

Marguerite Price, who cofounded the Community School, originally on De-Mun Avenue, wanted the interior of her new residence to have an Asian theme. The décor chosen for the sunroom was described as Chinese Modern. When the interior was completed, Marguerite invited Maritz & Young to see her creation. According to her actor son's reflection, "I think the architects never came back." Besides the many bedrooms, the paneled dining room, and the fully stocked library, the house had a grand stair in the main hall.

The front elevation of this Maritz & Young gem is composed of a projecting central bay at the main entrance with a classic wooden pediment over the doorway. A handsome Palladian-style window grouping above the entrance emphasizes the English theme of the house. A projecting band of brickwork continues around the house at the second-floor sill height. Double-hung windows dutifully appear in this design except at the attic dormers where casements are utilized. At either end of the front façade stands a projecting brick wall detail to the height of the second floor; on one end, this detail leads into a garden wall, on the other end it conceals a small entry into the house from the drive. At the rear of the house, a graceful central bay projects out from the structure extending the two full stories. The slate tile roof is distinctive in that the front and rear soffit continues around the house at both gable ends.

Continuing the pattern of skipping a house brings one to a Tudor Revival adaptation in rough stucco and brick. This is the **Edwin Meissner House**. Meissner was born in Milwaukee in 1884. As a teenager he worked as a messenger for the Milwaukee Electric Railway and Light Company. He came to St. Louis for a job at the St. Louis Car Company and in little more than a decade was president. The business was one of the largest manufacturers of railroad cars. Meissner was also president of the St. Louis Crime Commission, which he helped establish. He died in his home in 1956 while still president of the car company. Meissner contributed his free time to the Central Institute for the Deaf, the St. Louis Board of Police Commissioners, and New Mt. Sinai Cemetery, where he is now buried.

The Edwin Meissner House

The Edwin Meissner House, living room (above) and bedroom (below)

THE EDWIN MEISSNER HOUSE,
PLAYROOM (ABOVE) AND STAIR
HALL (LEFT)

The Meissner Tudor Revival–style residence is very similar to the Friedman house down the block. Like the Friedman residence, the exterior construction consists of irregular brickwork at the first floor with stucco and brick window surrounds at the second floor. The three gables on the front façade create an interesting composition, with the more delicate brick diamond-shaped design in contrast to the heavy timber oriel projecting over the main entrance. At the first floor, irregular brickwork extends around the house and frames the leaded glass casement windows. A brick chimney consisting of four flues reaches over the random slate roof. A small covered porch extends over the kitchen entry on one side of the house. Beyond the parking court, a sturdy timber porch extends out from a bedroom, echoing the large bay above the main entrance.

The entrance hall with its flagstone floor leads to the curved stairs sweeping up to the second floor. The hall opens to the living room through a modified Gothic arched opening rendered in cut stone. The fireplace, wood-beamed ceiling, and end wall of bookcases give a feeling of substance and security. The living room gives way to the dining room and then on through to the oval-shaped sunroom. A special feature of this home is the playroom located in the basement with a durable terrazzo floor and heavy timber ceiling with exposed hardware.

Today the Meissner residence is home to Forsyth School along with the neighboring house, also designed by Maritz & Young and once owned by another Edwin, Edwin Meyer. Much like his neighbors Friedman, Blackmer, Lewin,

The Edwin Meyer House

The Architecture of Maritz & Young

and Bush, Edwin Meyer worked for the family businesses owned by his father, George. Most prominent was the Meyer-Schmid Grocery Company located in the Cupples Station complex on South Seventh Street. Meyer and his wife, Frances, raised three daughters.

The **Edwin Meyer House**, the final Maritz & Young residence on Forsyth, was constructed in 1927. This brick residence of Norman and English design is recessed slightly farther from the street than its neighbors, owing to the garage wing projecting forward from the main house. The attached garage with its blind brick arcade is reminiscent of the John O'Fallon Jr. House in Brentmoor Park. This one-and-a-half-story wing is ringed with a series of Gothic arches with casements centered in each. The stair tower with the entry below rises up at the center of the right angle. Triple brick chimneys, each rotated to produce a more massive effect, extend above the roof and stair tower providing a picturesque composition. From various viewing angles one can admire the many roof ridges not fully appreciated from the street side alone.

Upon entering the rough plastered stair hall, a checkered terrazzo floor spreads out ahead with a graceful curving stair leading up to the second floor.

THE EDWIN MEYER HOUSE, LIVING ROOM
(ABOVE) AND GALLERY (LEFT)

The wood-paneled living room includes an elegant carved stone fireplace and rectangular bay at the far end. Next to the living room, the sun gallery is accessed through double arches and wrought-iron gates. A feature in the sun gallery is a built-in fountain set below a series of leaded glass windows. The sun gallery also connects to a dining room with a large bay at the rear set beyond a wide arched opening. The second floor consists of four family bedrooms and two baths with an additional bath and two bedrooms for servants.

Around Clayton

Besides the numerous Maritz & Young houses on West Brentmoor, Carrswold, and Forsyth, another locale with multiple residences is Southmoor Drive. The Roy Atwood House, one of the first designed by Maritz & Henderson, and the Roy Scholz House (constructed in 1917) are similar brick Georgian Revival gems, differentiated by the bay windows at the first floor of the Atwood house versus the round-topped windows and central roof dormer of the Scholz house. Scholz was a Washington University–educated physician with a downtown private practice. Louis Rosen, president of Rosen-Reichardt Brokerage Company, had his own Georgian-style residence constructed five years later, after Henderson had left the firm. Perhaps the most unusual house on the block is the Leo Rassieur House. Rassieur, an attorney and judge, had a beautiful Spanish-inspired house built at the northern entrance to the neighborhood.

The Forsyth-Wydown Historic District includes thirty-four Maritz & Young houses on Forsyth Boulevard, Alexander Drive, Cecil Avenue, Fauquier Drive, University Lane, Wydown Terrace, and Ellenwood Avenue. The land south of Ellenwood was owned by Thomas Skinker (1805–1887); the street is named for his "Ellenwood" home, which burned in 1900. The most significant Maritz & Young house on Ellenwood Avenue is the **Dr. Max Myer House**.

The 1926 Myer House has an English influence, noticeable in the architectural detailing including the brick diaper work in the gables, the oriel above the front entrance, and the classic chimney designs. The brickwork utilizes hard burnt headers to add interest within the field of the exterior walls. Wood shutters against the painted brick soften the overall feel of the house. On the garden side, a scalloped top wall encloses the parking court.

Surgeon Max Myer attended the University of Missouri before becoming a medical doctor at the Marion-Sims College of Medicine in St. Louis. He followed with postgraduate work in Germany and Austria. Dr. Myer relocated to St. Louis to run a general practice. The house was not commissioned by Dr. Myer, but by Alma Drey, a widow who married Dr. Myer before the house was completed. Alma later became a local historian with an interest in medical history. Dr. Myer lived in the house until his death in 1948 at the age of seventy.

THE DR. MAX MYER HOUSE, FRONT
(ABOVE) AND STAIR HALL (LEFT)

The house revolves around the
main hall, where to the right is the
living room, straight ahead is the
dining room and adjacent breakfast room, and to the left is the
main stair connecting three levels. A covered porch extends off
both the living and dining rooms
for casual summer eating. Beyond
the requisite pantry and kitchen,
a two-car garage is integrated into
the first floor.

On the second-floor level,
there are four family bedrooms,

three baths, and a sitting room with a fireplace. Two maids' rooms and a bath complete the plan. More usable space can be found in the attic with two finished bedrooms and another bath. Down on the basement level, a wood-beamed ceiling and a fireplace highlight a playroom. One more bedroom and bath here increases the tally to a total of nine finished bedrooms in this home.

Three additional Maritz & Young houses on Ellenwood Avenue, all constructed in 1922, were built for Hugh Scott, Oliver Anderson, and John Lionberger. Friends Anderson and Lionberger lived in similar Georgian Revival houses of brick construction. Their neighbor, Hugh Scott, was the founder of Western Machinery, later renamed Western Diesel Company.

—⁓—

The **Ralph Weil House** on University Lane is a relatively modest two-story French Norman Revival–style residence constructed in 1925. Hip roofs extend over an offset L-shaped plan with a stair tower rising within the two wings. Multiple segmental arched casement windows and French doors fill the whitewashed brick elevations. The projecting kitchen roofline is set somewhat lower than that of the living room with its smaller scaled windows, adding to the charm of the composition.

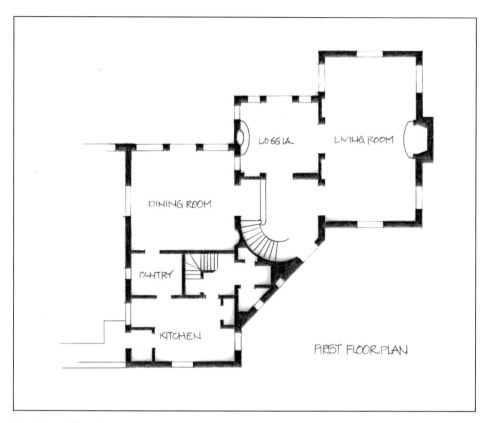

THE RALPH WEIL HOUSE, FIRST-FLOOR PLAN

THE RALPH WEIL HOUSE

The main stair hall is accessed through the angled entry under a circular stairway. The living room is to the right, the dining room to the left, with a loggia connecting the two. Both the living room and the master bedroom, directly above on the second floor, have fireplaces. At the second floor, the stair hall takes on a circular shape with a total of five bedrooms and three baths. The garage is in the basement along with a laundry room.

Weil Clothing Company was founded by Max Weil and his son Ralph. Ralph served in the U.S. Army Medical Corps in World War I. In 1919, while still in Paris, he married Nadia Cherdakoff. He came back to St. Louis and resumed work in the family business. When his father died a few years later, Ralph became president at the age of thirty. Weil pioneered many employee programs common today by offering health and insurance benefits and a retirement fund. He and Nadia were members of countless civic organizations and clubs; she contributing much of her time during World War II to organizations such as the American Red Cross. Weil died of heart failure in his Maritz & Young home in 1952.

Next door to Weil was the **Morris Rosenthal House**. Rosenthal was named a city judge in 1953 by St. Louis mayor Raymond Tucker, resigning twelve years later to work in private practice. Rosenthal was appointed again in 1973, this time by Mayor John Poelker. His residence is typical of the Tudor style: half-timbering, steeply pitched roof, casement windows, arched doors.

Perpendicular to University Lane is Cecil Avenue, with three additional Maritz & Young houses of varying styles. The Gustav Biston House is a French-Italian design with a rough stucco façade with large arched openings. Another Gustav down the street, Gustav Riesmeyer Jr., a vice president with First National Bank, preferred a Tudor-style house dominated by a projecting gable filled with a large nine-sectioned window. Across the street was a far simpler design for the Francis Muckerman House, a mixture of styles that tends toward the French with its shutters and wrought-iron.

THE MORRIS ROSENTHAL HOUSE, STAIR HALL

THE MORRIS ROSENTHAL HOUSE

William Ridgely Young and his wife, Elizabeth, first began looking at properties for their new home in 1921. Elizabeth wrote in her diary on April 1, 1921, that she went "out to see lots in Wydown with Johnny and Itchie."

They settled in the Wydown Terrace neighborhood, with twelve other Maritz & Young–designed houses. These are modest homes compared to Brentmoor, Carrswold, and Forsyth. Constructed between 1921 and 1926, the houses vary in style: the Georgian house of Harry Papin, descendant of St. Louis founder Pierre Laclede; Mary Scullin Green's French Revival home; the beautiful Tudor Revival–style Paul Lungstras residence; and the Spanish-influenced Clark Gamble, Julia Klein, and William Schock houses.

Wydown Terrace was designed by landscape architect John Noyes, who later laid out the grounds at Westwood Country Club, where Maritz & Young designed the clubhouse and several residences. The sunken common ground area fronting the neighborhood at Wydown Boulevard was once part of Arrowhead Lake, used during the World's Fair as part of the Philippine Reservation.

THE MARY SCULLIN GREEN HOUSE

The Paul Lungstras House (above) and the Julia Klein House (below)

To see how a Maritz & Young architect lived, examine the **William Ridgely Young House**. "Moving Day!" Elizabeth Young announces in her diary on June 18, 1923. On the following day she writes, "Sitting in my mansion surrounded by workmen." Despite Elizabeth's journalistic claims of a large house, the Ridgely Young house is a charming Spanish Eclectic abode relatively modest in scale. The flagstone driveway leads to a one-car garage that opens at both ends. The brightly colored Spanish roof tiles cap a stucco façade punctuated by French doors, with wrought-iron balconies on the second floor. A large flagstone terrace outside the living room blends seamlessly into its surroundings.

The cruciform layout is dominated on the first floor by the two-story sunken living room. A heavy timber vaulted ceiling soars above French doors with glass circular transoms bringing a significant amount of light into the room. A fireplace is on the far end and a beautiful staircase with a balcony above is near the entrance hall on the opposite side. Classic rough stucco walls permeate the house.

THE WILLIAM RIDGELY YOUNG HOUSE

THE WILLIAM RIDGELY YOUNG HOUSE,
LIVING ROOM (ABOVE AND RIGHT)

Although the house lacks a dining room, it has a loggia or sunroom with a vaulted ceiling and seven French doors. The second floor, which looks down into the living room, consists of two bedrooms, a dressing room, a bathroom, and a sleeping porch over the garage.

Elizabeth moved from the house when the couple divorced in 1929. She died in St. Louis in 1992. Ridgely

THE WILLIAM RIDGELY YOUNG HOUSE, LOGGIA (ABOVE) AND FIRST-FLOOR PLAN (LEFT)

Young remained in the house a few additional years before moving in with his sister Helon in the home he had designed in 1914 at 3232 Longfellow Boulevard. Several families have owned this house since Young.

Besides the Maritz & Henderson commissions in University City's Parkview and Ames Place, Maritz & Young designed several residences just north of Clayton on Westmoreland Drive and Maryland Avenue in University City. These houses are part of the Maryland Terrace Historic District. Raymond Jr. and James Maritz lived a block apart in houses constructed in 1920 and 1921, respectively. Between the brothers on Maryland Avenue was the modest traditional house of Herbert Piou. Piou, educated in Germany, came to America and was a partner in Sears & Piou, a steel sash and wire fence company. He was later president of Burroughs Glass Company. Two doors down was a small traditional house designed in 1921 and owned by architect Ridgely Young; he sold it a year later.

Two other houses located next door to each other on Westmoreland Drive belonged to Frank Ackerman and George Bayle. Bayle's Tudor Revival house, built in 1929, was a solid brick structure with a gable-roofed bay projecting toward the street, while the Ackerman home was a symmetrical Georgian Revival constructed the following year. Frank Ackerman was a vice president at Curtis Manufacturing Company when Walter Hecker (his house is profiled in the Brentmoor Park section) was president of the company.

Another Maritz & Young house farther down Westmoreland Drive is the Raymond Stahlberg House. This distinctive Spanish Eclectic home has a textured stucco façade with a projecting bay under a gable roof. Finally, there were two houses designed for Ridgely Young's father-in-law, Frank Nulsen, on Westmoreland Drive. Nulsen never lived in either house; he quickly sold the houses after construction.

Ladue, Missouri

The City of Ladue was incorporated in 1936 when the Village of Ladue merged with the villages of Deer Creek and McKnight. People had been living on the land for a hundred years before the incorporation. The almost-nine-square-mile town is one of the wealthiest in America. The city was named for Ladue Road, which led to property owned by Peter Ladue, who had possession of two hundred acres in the mid-1800s, though he may never have lived in the area. He was a land speculator who left St. Louis after a lawsuit and is not considered the founder of the village.

St. Louis Country Club

St. Louis Country Club, the first private country club in St. Louis, was founded in 1896 and originally located on Hanley Road in Clayton. The clubhouse, replaced the following year after a fire destroyed the original, was surrounded by a golf course, polo grounds, and stables. The club moved to Ladue in 1914 after purchasing more than two hundred acres from the St. Louis Archdiocese; seventy-five acres were allotted for residential development. The golf course hosted the U.S. Amateur (1921) and the Women's Amateur (1925), but gained prominence by hosting the 1947 U.S. Open Golf Championship where Lew Worsham defeated Sam Snead in an eighteen-hole playoff.

The clubhouse was designed by Mauran, Russell & Crowell in the Spanish Eclectic style. Landscape architect Henry Wright, who also planned the Brentmoor neighborhood, was responsible for laying out the residential lots at the club. The buyers were required to choose lot numbers from a hat and were not allowed to trade them. Raymond Maritz's former partner, Gale Henderson, designed six residences on the country club grounds. In 2011, the St. Louis Country Club neighborhood was ranked fourth among "The 25 Richest Neighborhoods in America" on the website *Business Insider*.

Maritz & Young designed the 1929 Tudor Revival **Edwin Nugent House** with many of the classic characteristics: stucco façade, half-timber gables, multiple projecting bays, large chimney, oriel windows, and a slate roof. The house has ten thousand square feet of living space. Today, much of this residence is concealed from the street. Following Nugent's death in 1934, his widow lived in the house until her death in 1963.

Edwin Nugent was vice president of Douglas Loan & Investment Company. He was the son of Byron Nugent, wealthy founder of B. Nugent & Bro. Dry Goods Company. The family lived at 29 Westmoreland Place. When Edwin Nugent died of pneumonia, his funeral took place in his St. Louis Country Club home.

One of the many residences lining the golf course is the **Donaldson Lambert House**. Donaldson was the grandson of Jordan Lambert, who founded Lambert Pharmaceutical Company and made his fortune manufacturing Listerine. He was also the eldest son of Major Albert Bond Lambert, aviation pioneer, financial backer of Charles Lindbergh's *Spirit of St. Louis*, and founder of Lambert Airport. The major lived nearby on Cella Road. Donaldson was an executive at the pharmaceutical firm. He and his wife, Caroline, sold their Maritz & Young house

THE EDWIN NUGENT HOUSE

THE DONALDSON LAMBERT HOUSE (ABOVE) AND SITE PLAN (BELOW)

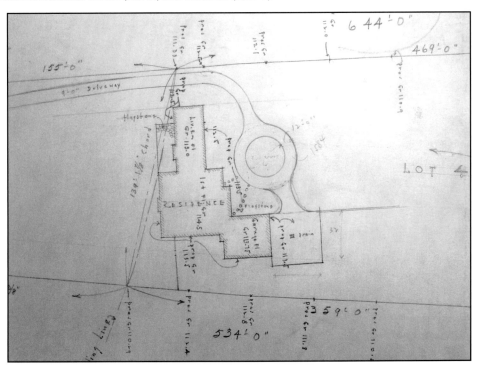

in 1936. Both died in a fire at their home on Westmoreland Place in December 1968. It wasn't the first family tragedy; in 1929, Donaldson's brother George had died in a plane crash while giving a flying lesson.

THE DONALDSON LAMBERT HOUSE, LIVING ROOM

Three brick chimneys rise upward in the front elevation of this 1928 English-style residence. Brickwork, timber lintels, and wood siding in the gables are all painted. The main entrance is through a recessed covered porch. Through the main hall, directly ahead, another covered porch shelters a garden side entrance. The sunken living room has a rustic feel with a beamed ceiling overhead that complements the exposed brick hearth and fireplace. The sunroom opens up at the end of the living room with three arched openings containing French doors to the outside.

Looking back through to the main hall, the primary stairs can be seen leading up to the second floor. The formal dining room is fitted with a small corner fireplace. Beyond this is the breakfast room, accessible through either the dining room or the pantry. Besides the kitchen, a guest bedroom and bath fill out the first floor. An attached garage wing includes a man's room and bath and rear stair for the two maids' rooms and bath above. On the second floor of the main house, a master bedroom suite contains a bath, a dressing room, a sleeping porch, and a fireplace. There are two additional bedrooms, two baths, a nursery and small sleeping room, and a sleeping porch. The basement includes a den space with its own fireplace.

A short distance down the road is the **Clifton McMillan House**, rendered in a Georgian Revival style. This brick home's façade is asymmetrical, with the entrance bay to the left of center. Its pediment extends above the stone quoins surrounding the main door with brick quoins defining the corners of the residence. Regularly spaced windows line both the first and second floors with lighter colored solid shutters at the first floor and darker colored louvered shutters at the smaller second-floor windows. A Colonial-inspired service wing extends at an angle from the main house to the garage. The garden elevation reveals a more irregular composition including a gabled bay and a three-sided bay. A graceful, lightly scaled stairway leads to the second floor from the entrance hall. To the right is the paneled living room detailed with plaster cornices and decorative wood moldings.

Clifton McMillan came to St. Louis from Bowling Green, Missouri. He worked various positions at Hammett-Anderson-Wade Realty. When the busi-

The Clifton McMillan House

The Clifton McMillan House, stair hall (above) and study (below)

THE CLIFTON MCMILLAN HOUSE, LIVING ROOM

ness merged with Mercantile Trust Company, McMillan was elected secretary and director; he later became vice president of the Mercantile-Commerce Bank & Trust Company. He resigned his position in 1931 and died the following year. His wife, Anne, lived in the house for many years.

Nearby stands the **Samuel Plant House**. Samuel Plant (1872–1953) spent his entire career at the family business, George P. Plant Milling Company. His father also founded the Franklin Flour Mill. Plant first worked as a miller before moving up the ranks from vice president and general manager to president in 1918. The business was sold eight years later. According to *The Book of St. Louisans* (1912), Plant enjoyed hunting and motoring. He was married to Claire Ewing, a descendant of St. Louis founder Pierre Laclede. His mother was Alby Easton, daughter of Alton Easton, for whom Alton, Illinois, is named.

This two-story Tudor Revival has a rustic feel with its rough stonework, stucco, heavy timber details, and random slate roof. Adding to the charm are the roof ridges turning up at the gable ends. Shed roof dormers rise up at various elevations contributing to the modest scaling of the house. Stone corbels and brackets contrast with the random stonework and stucco finishes. At the garden elevation, a gallery half open and half enclosed is supported by timber posts with an outdoor deck at the second floor.

THE SAMUEL PLANT HOUSE, FIRST-FLOOR PLAN

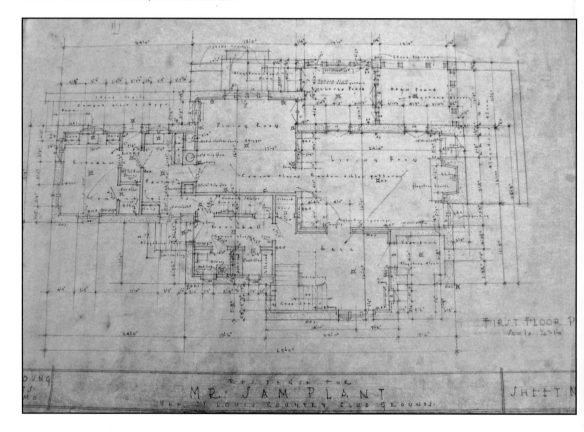

SAMUEL PLANT (RIGHT) AND THE SAMUEL
PLANT HOUSE, GARDEN VIEW (ABOVE)

Entry is through a covered vestibule into the stair hall. The living room maintains the rustic flavor, floors are of cement in a random ashlar pattern, and a flagstone hearth anchors the fireplace at one end of the room. Adjacent to the living room is a covered porch, half of which is enclosed and connected to the dining room. A pantry and kitchen extend beyond the dining room with a small exterior deck serving the kitchen and dining room. On the second floor of this 1924 house are three family bedrooms, each with a window seat, two having direct access to an open porch deck. Above the service wing, there are an additional two maids' rooms. Garage facilities are located in the basement.

Situated on the far side of the golf course from the other Maritz & Young residences is the modestly scaled English cottage–style **Heman Pettengill House**.

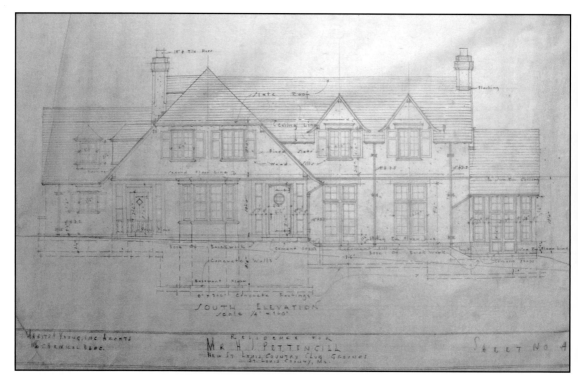

THE HEMAN PETTENGILL HOUSE, FRONT ELEVATION

The one-and-a-half-story structure is in stucco and half-timber work with a combination of both gabled and modified hip roof design. Painted wood shutters accent the elevations, framing many of the window openings. Eyebrow dormers extend above the gutter line.

The entrance of the residence is through a covered porch into a main hall. The living room, situated to the right, has four pairs of French doors allowing light into the room with its built-in bookcases and fireplace. Beyond, down several steps, is a sunroom with a complement of French doors, a fireplace situated back to back with that of the living room, and a small garden pool. A breakfast room lies directly ahead in the main hall. To the left of the entrance is the dining room, with a projecting bay and wood cornice. A small covered porch can be accessed from the dining room opposite from the main entry porch. The kitchen and a two-car garage complete the first floor. Up a simple enclosed staircase are three family bedrooms and two baths, along with two maids' rooms and a bath over the attached garage.

Heman Pettengill was born in Maine. He spent his career working in the telegraph, and later the telephone, business. His first job was with Western Union Telegraph Company in 1875. Pettengill moved up the corporate ladder at American Rapid Telegraph Company and Postal Telegraph Cable Company before accepting the presidency of Southwestern Telegraph and Telephone in Dallas, Texas. His final move was to St. Louis where he was president and later chairman of Southwestern Bell Telephone. Pettengill and his first wife had three children; he remarried several years after his first wife's death. His favorite pastime was playing golf at St. Louis Country Club.

Mahlon Wallace Jr. acquired his St. Louis Country Club land through his parents when they purchased forty acres and parceled it out to their children in 1924. However, the name on the architectural drawings for the **Mahlon Wallace Jr. House** is Edward A. Faust, Wallace's father-in-law. Faust and his wife, Anna Louise Busch, daughter of Adolphus Busch, commissioned the house for the Wallaces.

Wallace and his wife, Audrey, named their home "Casa Audlon," a combination of their first names. He was president and chairman of Wallace Pencil Company (previously run by his father, Mahlon Sr.) and the Wallace Corporation, a conglomerate manufacturing clothespins, toothpicks, and paper food trays. He

The Mahlon Wallace Jr. House, garden view

THIS PAGE: THE MAHLON
WALLACE JR. HOUSE, LOGGIA
(ABOVE) AND SITE PLAN (LEFT).
FACING PAGE: LIVING ROOM.

worked to establish
the St. Louis County
Library system and
was president of the
Library Association
until 1970. While
Wallace was an ex-
cellent polo player
and avid hunter, Audrey excelled in golf as the five-time winner of the St. Louis
Women's Invitational Golf Championship. She remained in the house until her
death in 1991.

Here is an example of a Mediterranean style hearkening back to both Spanish and Italian influences. Constructed in 1924, the residence is designed in the shape of a cross. Stone accents, carved wood lintels, and brick sills feature throughout the rustic stucco elevations. Delicate wrought-ironwork contrasts with wood posts and capitals of the covered porch supported by projecting vaulting. A variety of window designs continues all around the residence, ranging from classic French doors to arched casements to pierced opening or grille combinations. An unusual feature to this residence is an open exterior stair leading to a second-floor roof deck.

The residence is entered through a circular vestibule near the center. Moving clockwise, beginning at the top of the cross, is the dining room, and beyond is a vaulted sunroom with a fireplace. At the three o'clock position, just above the vestibule, is the two-story living room with another fireplace on the far wall; the arched wood-beamed ceiling and the sunken floor give the room a massive feel. Six small round windows of leaded glass are located near the ceiling. The bot-

THE MAHLON WALLACE JR. HOUSE, HUNTING ROOM

tom of the cross consists of a hunting room, as labeled in the *Monograph* books, or a gun room, as the drawings label it. This space has a stone floor, decorative beamed ceiling, five small windows facing each other on either side, and a third fireplace on the first floor. The final wing at nine o'clock consists of the kitchen and service quarters; this is the longest wing of the cross. The center of the house contains a pantry and two staircases. The living room is open to the second floor, which consists of three bedrooms, two baths, two fireplaces, a large dressing room, and two walkout terraces.

Around Ladue

The **Edmund O'Donnell House** on Ladue Road is the second Maritz & Young house for this homeowner; the first residence of nearly the same design is on Alexander Drive in Clayton, where the family lived for five years. Roof ridges turning upward toward the ends gives this modest Tudor Revival home a rustic sense of age. Stucco with stone and brick detailing complement the massive timberwork. Additional exterior details include board-and-batten-style shutters, wrought-iron-work, a substantial projecting bay on the east elevation, and a porte-cochere connecting to the garage.

The small entry opening onto the main stair landing leads down to the main floor into the two-story living room. Exposed timberwork, a stone fireplace, an open stairway, and a large bank of windows contribute to the character of this space. Turned wood posts separate the dining room from the living room. French

THE EDMUND O'DONNELL HOUSE

The Edmund O'Donnell House, living room (above) and rear elevation (below)

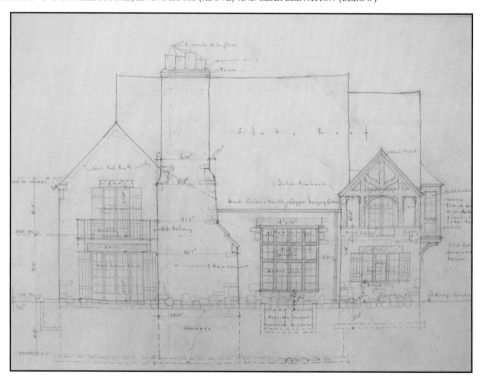

THE EDMUND O'DONNELL HOUSE, BEDROOM

doors provide access to the garden outside. Completing the first floor are the pantry, kitchen, and small maids' room and bath at the entry.

At the top of the open-sided stairs, a beautiful master bedroom suite features a steeply vaulted wood ceiling, a fireplace, an exterior balcony, and a bath. Backtracking across the balcony overlooking the living room is a second bedroom and bath with its own enclosed sleeping porch.

Edmund O'Donnell was vice president and secretary of his father's company, E. R. O'Donnell Mercantile on Olive Street. He was also on the board of Falstaff Brewing and president of Valentine Warehouse Company. O'Donnell and his wife, Florence, who had four children, were friends of Ridgely Young and his wife. O'Donnell was only forty-eight years old when he passed away of pneumonia in 1943.

Sited on a hillside just off of Ladue Road is the 1927 French Norman–style **Arnold Stifel House**. Painted rustic brickwork and shutters contrast with half-timber and stucco elements. Arched windows and dormers, wrought-ironwork, and decorative chimneys add to the elegant look of the home. A two-

THE ARNOLD STIFEL HOUSE, FRONT ELEVATION (ABOVE) AND GARDEN VIEW (BELOW)

ARNOLD STIFEL (ABOVE) AND A DRAWING OF
HIS HOME (RIGHT)

story entrance tower is detailed with cut stone window surround. The hip roofs
and gable roofs at varying ridge heights give the impression that this structure
could have evolved over time. In reality, additions were originally anticipated
and were detailed in 1940, yielding additional bathrooms, two bedrooms and a
unique semi-recessed covered porch. Timber ceilings span both the living and
dining rooms with a vaulted timber ceiling in the master bedroom.

Arnold Stifel was the retired president and chairman of investment banking firm Stifel, Nicolaus & Company. The business was cofounded by his father,
Herman. Arnold joined the firm in the 1920s and rode the ups and downs of
the prosperous 1920s and Depression-era 1930s. He resigned in 1941 after the
death of his father. Much like his fellow Maritz & Young homeowners, Stifel was
active in charity and civic organizations. Stifel's wife, Mildred, was the sister of
Percy Orthwein, D'Arcy Advertising president and chairman, and another Maritz
& Young client. The couple sold this Ladue home and moved into the Maritz &
Young–designed Lindell Boulevard former residence of Morton Jourdan.

THE FRED HERMANN HOUSE

English traditional describes the 1936 **Fred Hermann House** on Litzsinger Road. The colorful slate roof crowns a rustic painted brick façade with three gables on the entrance side. Brick lintels cover window openings and a brick dentil design follows around the second-floor line. Painted wood shutters soften the overall formality of the exterior. Wrought-iron panels support the entrance porch structure.

Fred's father, Louis, got into the tanning business in 1881, in part to supply wagon trains heading west. Fred began working for Hermann Oak Leather in 1907 and later became president of the company.

The visitor enters through a small arched vestibule into the stair hall. Directly ahead lies the living room with French doors on axis, opening to the outdoors. To the left are the main stair and an entrance to a first-floor bedroom, bath, and enclosed sleeping porch. The dining room and loggia connect directly with the living room. A screened porch accesses both the living and dining rooms, looking out to a reflecting pool on the terrace.

Three bedrooms and two baths serve the family on the second floor. Over the service wing are two maids' rooms and a bath. On the basement level is a wood-paneled recreation room with a fireplace. One additional bedroom and bath is provided for the resident chauffeur and handyman. A separate three-car detached garage sits adjacent to the main house.

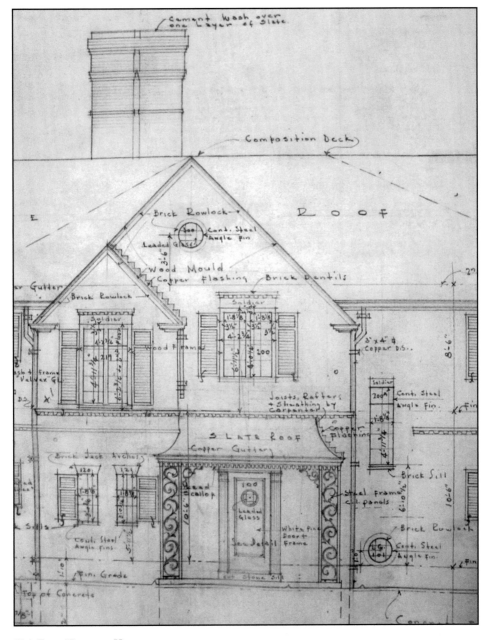

THE FRED HERMANN HOUSE, FRONT ELEVATION

The **Frank Mayfield House** gradually descends down its sloping site. Every elevation of this fine, rambling Tudor Revival is full of charm and character. Rustic stonework and slate roofing characterize this picturesque house accented by timber, stucco, and brickwork. Multiple steeply pitched gables bring the roofline snugly below the second-floor ceiling line, creating dormers at many second-floor window openings. The separate garage with its apartment above is topped with a dovecote cupola and distinctive wrought-iron weathervane.

The Frank Mayfield House (above)
and stair hall (left)

A deep entry vestibule leads into the main hall and stretches to the rear of the house. To the right, a beautiful cantilevered circular staircase rises to the second floor, revealing massive timberwork supporting the balcony above. The tower ceiling is in timber, supporting a wrought-iron chandelier at the center point of the stairway. The formal dining room, with its carved stone fireplace dominating one wall, is situated up two steps, beyond wrought-iron gates. An exterior covered breakfast porch leads off from both the main dining room and the butler's pantry. Rounding out the service side is a servants' dining room, the kitchen, and the laundry room. To the left of the hall, the living room is down more steps. The heavy timber beamed ceiling, stone fireplace, paneled walls, and deep bay add to the warmth of this room. Another stair hall with a circular staircase leads farther down to a secluded library, which is situated at an angle from the main house. A

fireplace, oak floors, timber ceiling, and built-in bookcases are featured in this room. On two walls, access to a covered porch is provided by French doors. At the front of the house, a playroom for the children is accessed by way of its own separate passageway running parallel to the living room. Another covered porch is located at the end of this passageway.

As with the first floor, the second floor gradually steps down from right to left. The owner's bedroom suite has access to two bathrooms. Noteworthy is the breakfast room outside of the owner's bedroom, which includes a fireplace and small kitchenette. A child's bedroom (with its own sleeping porch) and two guest bedrooms each contain a fireplace. A nurse's room and three servants' rooms share a bath. Over the library, through the second, smaller stair hall, is a separate suite containing its own bath, fireplace, and sleeping porch.

Frank Mayfield, a native of Cleveland, Tennessee, attended Vanderbilt University and worked in banking before serving in the infantry reserves during World War I, though he was not sent overseas. He and his wife, Juanita, had two children; Juanita was a founder of the Community School and a director of Mary Institute. Mayfield went back to banking briefly, then came to St. Louis to work for his father-in-law, M. L. Wilkinson, who was president of Scruggs-Vandervoort-Barney Dry Goods Company, one of the largest department store chains in the Midwest. Mayfield took over the presidency upon Wilkinson's death in 1925. Under his leadership, the department store business grew from two to fourteen stores. He published *The Department Store Story*, a book about his life in the business, in 1948. He served on the boards of many community and business organizations including the Chamber of Commerce and the Municipal Theater Association. Frank Mayfield died during the bicentennial year of 1976.

Mayfield had previously owned a Maritz & Young house in the same Wydown Terrace neighborhood as that of architect Ridgely Young. This Tudor-style residence, built in 1921, was a modest L-shaped stucco structure with a slate roof. The Mayfields sold this house in 1924.

Oliver Anderson owned two Maritz & Young houses, his first constructed in 1924 in Clayton, followed by the 1927 **Oliver Anderson House** in Ladue. Rustic painted brickwork defines this Tudor Revival with projecting headers sprinkled throughout each of the elevations. Two steep gables stand out from the main house, allowing a recessed arched entry. To the left, two lightly scaled brick flues, on a diagonal, extend above the main chimney structure. Adding to the vignette, a small box bay extends out from the second floor. Garden walls contain the parking court between the residence and the story-and-a-half garage. The garden elevation reveals an enclosed porch and short gallery in timber at the second floor. There are two different-sized shallow hipped bays at either side of the main cross gable.

Anderson managed Oliver J. Anderson & Company, an investment securities firm. In 1928, before a dinner and reception celebrating Charles Lindbergh and his flight across the Atlantic, the aviator gave ten-minute flights to prominent St. Louisans including Oliver Anderson and his wife. In 1931, Anderson was on his way to a hunt club in St. Charles, Missouri, along with his friends Harold Bixby, former president of the Chamber of Commerce and a financial supporter of Charles Lindbergh's *Spirit of St. Louis*; Edgar Queeny, president of Monsanto

THE OLIVER ANDERSON HOUSE, FRONT (TOP) AND GARDEN VIEW (BELOW)

Chemical Company; and Harry Hall Knight, another Lindbergh backer and broker in his own firm. Knight was driving when his car swung off the highway, hit an embankment, and turned over. A broken steering rod was determined to have caused the accident. Anderson was the only fatality. He left behind a wife and three children.

A Glimpse: The Lost Art of Drafting

One of the great pleasures of researching this book was the opportunity to again review the original Maritz & Young drawings. As a former employee of Raymond E. Maritz & Sons, Inc., the descendant firm of Maritz & Young, I was familiar with the drawings but had not seen them in many years. I began a summer internship in 1973 and fondly remember the venerable semi-retired Raymond Maritz Sr. arriving and greeting everyone before walking to his office. At the time, I didn't appreciate the quality of the architectural designs produced by him and his firm fifty years earlier.

Perhaps the foremost thought in my mind as I examined the drawings recently was how the modern creation of technical drawings has changed. Architectural drafting, or technical drawing, is becoming a lost art as architectural and engineering firms have replaced drafting tables, T-squares, triangles, and lead pencils with computerized CAD systems by which lines are created simply by clicking a mouse. Today, technical drawing is rarely included in any architectural school curriculum.

In the past, architectural firms prided themselves on the elegance and consistency of their drawings. There was a beauty to the flow from an ink pen or lead pencil along the edge of a T-square or triangle connecting exact points on a sheet of linen or vellum. The result was a precise form of communication, giving instructions to a builder on how to create a three-dimensional structure out of a two-dimensional representation. Like carving a sculpture, the drafting pencil created an image out of nothing—a distinctive floor plan, a towering elevation, a precise stair detail. Hand drawings produce a character and depth to the finished work, a quality ultimately lacking in a simple computer drawing. A fine lettering style would be mandated to produce a set of cohesive looking drawings yielding the signature of a single author. Today, the personal lettering style of every draftsman has been extinguished by the common keyboard.

The Maritz & Young drawings are sketched on thin vellum paper, except for a few earlier works by Maritz & Henderson that were completed on gray linen sheets penned in black ink. Examining the drawings was like revisiting

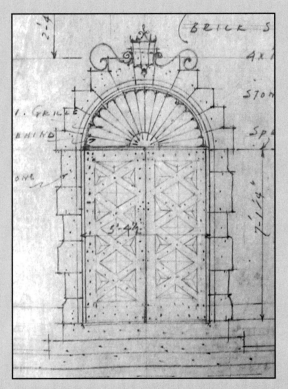

THE FREDERICK MEYER HOUSE, DOOR DETAIL

old friends, bringing back the nostalgia of these great residences. I was again impressed by both the quality of the drafting and the architectural lettering of a time past. I speculated if Raymond Maritz had drawn a particular floor plan, or if Ridgely Young had completed the splendid elevation, or if it was one of the draftsmen who had plied their talents when the firm was in its heyday. Full-scale drawings of selected details such as wrought-iron work or mantelpieces seemed to allow the draftsman to show off his skill. In many instances, I found simple cursive comments written on a plan or detail that indicated a change of thought or question. Repeatedly, I witnessed the hand-signed name of Raymond Maritz, identifying the plans and designs from one of St. Louis's finest residential architectural firms.

—*L. John Schott, AIA*

The Maritz & Young houses for Adalbert von Gontard and Percy Orthwein are within walking distance of one another in Huntleigh, Missouri; one a beautiful country home near Lindbergh Boulevard, the other a grand mansion resting in the valley near its neighbor.

The **Adalbert von Gontard House** is another example of the Tudor Revival style. The house was purchased by von Gontard while it was under construction by E. L. Bakewell, the name listed on the Maritz & Young drawings. Situated below street level and overlooking a small valley below, the setting is evocative of the English countryside. Casement windows, many with timber lintels above, punctuate the painted brick exterior walls. The main entry is set below a tall stair window pushing above the simple roofline. A charming stucco and half-timber box bay supported on timber brackets adds interest to the rear elevation. Carriage doors indicate the two-car attached garage. Multiple outbuildings are sited below the main house, adding to the overall agrarian impression.

The main stair hall is open to the second floor. Cantilevered beams

Adalbert von Gontard

THE ADALBERT VON GONTARD HOUSE,
FRONT (ABOVE) AND STAIR HALL (RIGHT)

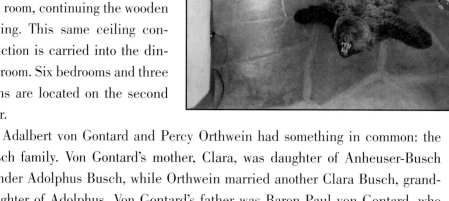

support the balconies above. Massive timber beams support smaller timber purlins (beams) and the wood floor above the living room. A generous covered porch extends off of the end of this room, continuing the wooden ceiling. This same ceiling construction is carried into the dining room. Six bedrooms and three baths are located on the second floor.

Adalbert von Gontard and Percy Orthwein had something in common: the Busch family. Von Gontard's mother, Clara, was daughter of Anheuser-Busch founder Adolphus Busch, while Orthwein married another Clara Busch, granddaughter of Adolphus. Von Gontard's father was Baron Paul von Gontard, who

THE ADALBERT VON GONTARD HOUSE,
LIVING ROOM (TOP), STABLE (ABOVE), AND
BEDROOM (RIGHT)

belonged to a prominent German industrial family. The baron became managing director of a Berlin ammunitions and weapons factory, Karlsruhe Industrial Works. He met Clara Busch in the German capital. The couple came to St. Louis to marry, but they returned to Berlin where they entertained German high society. He continued managing the munitions plant after World War I and was president of Mercedes-Benz & Manser Corporation of Stuttgart. After Hitler rose to power in 1933, the baron was arrested for transferring money to Holland and Switzerland. When freed by the Nazis, von Gontard moved to Zurich with Clara, where he died in 1941.

Adalbert or "Adie" von Gontard (1900–1976) came to the United States in 1923 to work at Anheuser-Busch; he was a chief engineer within a few years. He was one year younger than his cousin Gussie Busch. He left the brewery in 1955 as an officer and large shareholder. Adie was married to Susanne Schilling von Constatt; the couple had two sons and a daughter. They spent time at their home near Stuttgart, Germany, as well as their estate in Huntleigh, Missouri. Adie and Gussie Busch helped with the breeding and development of hounds for the Bridlespur Hunt Club, another Maritz & Young design that is currently a private residence.

THE BRIDLESPUR HUNT CLUB

Percy Orthwein (1888–1957) worked in myriad businesses, from advertising and beer production to railroads and coal mining. His father, William, was a wealthy pioneer grain merchant and president of Kinloch Telephone Company. Percy Orthwein is most associated with D'Arcy Advertising, where he would later become president and chairman of the board. He was educated at Yale and studied art in Heidelberg and Munich, Germany. In the ensuing years he became an accomplished illustrator and portrait painter. In 1916, he married Clara Busch,

daughter of Anheuser-Busch president August Busch Sr. and granddaughter of founder Adolphus Busch. The couple received a mansion on Lindell Boulevard as a wedding gift from her father. They moved to forty-eight acres in Huntleigh and their Maritz & Young house in 1930. Orthwein served on the boards of many corporations including Anheuser-Busch. He died in his Huntleigh home in 1957.

PERCY AND CLARA ORTHWEIN

Sitting on expansive acreage near the von Gontard residence is the **Percy Orthwein House**. This 1930 baronial residence placed in a country setting has a strong French influence, certainly when the garden elevation is viewed from a substantial distance through the trees. Slate-tiled hip roofs cap rustic stone walls throughout. A squared stair tower dominates the center bay at the entrance front. The entranceway itself is understated except for the glazed canopy projecting from the vestibule. Most of the windows and French door openings are framed with painted wood shutters.

The second-floor French doors are crowned with gables projecting above the gutter line, giving the effect of eyebrow dormers. The stone detailing is reminiscent of brickwork. Arched windows accented in cut stone connect the center bay with the two outer bays on both the entrance elevation and the garden side. Wrought-iron balconies at second-floor openings accent most elevations. Four stone chimneys anchor the residence in place.

The Percy Orthwein House, front (above) and garden view (below)

In the main hall, the circular stair rises from the basement level to the second floor. Ceilings within the main rooms are ten feet or more on both the first and second floors. Through a generous loggia is a forty-foot-long living room running front to back with no fewer than five sets of French door openings. The dining room is directly off of the main hall with its own fireplace; a spacious breakfast room is adjacent. A secluded study is tucked away near the service wing where the kitchen, pantry, servants' dining room, and a laundry room project from the main house.

Five family bedrooms are located on the second floor, with four baths and a sitting room. An additional two maids' rooms and a bath are located off the back hall. Above the laundry is a man's room and bath. The basement includes a stair hall and lounge with a ten-foot-high beamed ceiling, stone corbels, and fireplace; a children's playroom; and two half baths. A four-bay garage is sited across the entry lane away from the main house.

Maritz & Young also designed Huntleigh residences for Percy's sons, Adolphus and James Orthwein.

Near the von Gontard and Orthwein residences in Huntleigh is the **Leo Carton House**. Sitting prestigiously on a small rise is the French-influenced residence with a round Norman-style entrance tower and painted brick. Brick dentils carry around the house at the second-floor line. The entrance door framed with brick quoins is located off-center in the tower wall. The second-floor windows are either brick dormers projecting above the gutter line or true wood-framed dormers above the roof capped off with arched copper roofs. To the left of the tower, a second-floor porch is partially protected by a wrought-iron and copper standing seam roof. At the garden elevation, the garage wing is designed to appear as subordinate to the main house by means of a dropped cornice line, lowering the gutter line almost nine feet below that of the rest of the house.

THE LEO CARTON HOUSE, GARDEN VIEW

From the semicircular stair hall, the terrazzo stairs sweep up to the second floor. A fine, decorative wrought-iron railing rings the stairs and balcony above. The living room has French-inspired painted wood molding, a parquetry wood floor, a marble fireplace, built-in display cases, and electric wall sconces. A pair of doors leads to a screened porch. The dining room lies directly off of the stair hall in detail similar to the living room. A kitchen and pantry extend into the

THE LEO CARTON HOUSE, LIVING
ROOM (ABOVE) AND STAIR HALL (RIGHT)

service wing with two maids'
rooms and a bath over the
basement garage. On the second floor, a graceful balcony
connects three bedrooms, all
with vaulted ceilings, along
with a study and two baths.

Leo Carton was a St. Louis
native born in 1882. He attended Saint Louis University
and in 1911 married Dorothy
Shapleigh. Carton worked five
years for the National Bank of

Commerce before entering the brokerage business. He served in World War I and was a member of the Missouri Historical Society and the St. Louis Country Club.

The **Dr. A. G. Enderle House** is located in the Hampton Park Historic District in Richmond Heights just outside of the Clayton city limits. Adolph Gustavus Enderle came to St. Louis from Iowa and clerked at several drugstores before graduating from Missouri Medical College. The good doctor started his own drug business at Sixth and Chestnut streets and incorporated Enderle Drug Company. He was a member of the Missouri Athletic Club and the Mercantile Club. The doctor and his wife, Lillie, bought this property in 1928 and moved from the house a decade later. Dr. Enderle passed away in 1943.

Here is another pleasing example of Tudor Revival style in an ashlar stone at the first floor and brick at the second floor. Irregular stone quoins and window trim appear at the second-floor elevations. The projecting entrance bay is supported by buttress detailing at either side of the Gothic-style entrance door, which is itself highlighted by a large stone and brick surround design. Familiar heavy timber lintels span first-floor window openings. A quaint oriel appears at the second floor,

The Dr. A. G. Enderle House

THE DR. A. G. ENDERLE
HOUSE, STAIR HALL (ABOVE)
AND LIVING ROOM (LEFT)

just to the right of
the entrance bay.
On the garden side,
some stucco and
half-timber work is
showcased.

As one enters
the spacious main hall beneath the circular stairs, the sunroom lies directly ahead beyond wrought-iron gates, with the living room off to one side. The
beamed-ceiling living room crowns the space in a simple fashion with the carved
stone fireplace maintaining this same lean design. An outdoor terrace is accessed
through both the living room and the sunroom. A fountain is featured in this
outdoor setting. Back through the main hall is the dining room. Beyond is an

octagonal-shaped breakfast room that also is accessed through the sunroom. The pantry and kitchen round out the first floor. An attached two-car garage contains the stairs to the basement where a man's bedroom and bath are located. On the second floor are three bedrooms and two baths, with a maids' room and a bath over the garage. Two clothes chutes service the second floor.

The **Eugene Nims House** is located in Bee Tree Park in south St. Louis County. The stone elevation of this Tudor Revival gem stretches over eighty-seven feet with a recessed entrance to the left. The timber lintels over the windows complement the materials used in the two sleeping porches book-ending the residence. Projecting above the rustic slate roof is an interesting circular chimney of twisting brick. The flagstone patio outside the sunroom, which overlooks the Mississippi River, was undoubtedly a place where the family spent many an afternoon.

Eugene Nims was born in Fond du Lac, Wisconsin, eleven days after President Abra-

Right: Eugene Nims. Below: The Eugene Nims House, second-floor plan

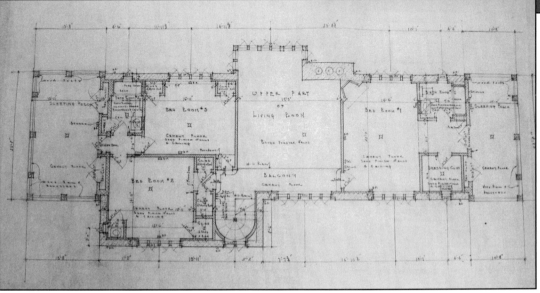

The Eugene Nims House

ham Lincoln's assassination. In Oklahoma he started his own lumber business before establishing three banks in the state. Nims got into public utilities by linking small towns by phone, and within eight years he had established the Pioneer Telephone and Telegraph Company. This company merged with two others to become the Southwestern Bell Telephone Company. Ultimately, he became president and chairman of the board and also served on the boards of many banks and insurance companies in the Midwest. He retired in 1932.

Nims married Lotawana Flateau in 1914. The couple had a city house in the fashionable Portland Place neighborhood. Nims also had a summer home called "The Larches" in Woods Hole, Massachusetts. In 1916, they purchased acreage sitting on this bluff above the Mississippi River about twenty miles south of St. Louis. They named their 192-acre estate "Bee Tree Farm" and built the Maritz & Young house in 1929. Nims suffered from Parkinson's disease and was confined to a wheelchair for years before his death in 1954. St. Louis County was able to purchase the farm after Lotawana Nims's death in 1966 through the efforts of the Open Space Council.

THE EUGENE NIMS HOUSE, LIVING ROOM

Inside, the fifty-foot long combination dining room/living room/sunroom dominates the first floor. Detailed wood-paneled walls give this space a stately yet comfortable feel. The living area opens upward two stories with a bay of windows on the river side of the house. A cantilevered balcony leads to the master bedroom suite on the second floor. This bedroom has a corner fireplace and access to a heavy timber sleeping porch. Another sleeping porch at the opposite end of the second floor accommodates the other two bedrooms. A kitchen with a dining alcove and a maids' room round out the first floor.

TOP: THE A. J. LEVY HOUSE, CLAYTON, 1928. BOTTOM: THE EUGENE ERKER HOUSE, CLAYTON, 1928.

The W. J. Schminke House,
Ladue, 1928, garden view
(above) and loggia (right)

THE WILLIAM MOYDELL HOUSE, IMPERIAL, MISSOURI, 1928, GARDEN VIEW (TOP) AND LOGGIA (BOTTOM)

Top: The Gustave Boehmer House, Ladue, 1938. Bottom: The T. Lewin House, Westwood Country Club grounds, St. Louis, 1936.

The Architecture of Maritz & Young

TOP: THE ALBERT STANNARD HOUSE, CREVE COEUR, MISSOURI, 1938. BOTTOM: THE ROY SIEGEL HOUSE, HUNTLEIGH, MISSOURI, DATE UNKNOWN.

THE
COMMERCIAL PROJECTS
OF
MARITZ & YOUNG

GALLERY OF COMMERCIAL PROJECTS

WHILE MARITZ & YOUNG SPECIALIZED primarily in residential architecture, they also contributed commercial designs to the St. Louis landscape. The photographs in this chapter document a few of their works, including the United Hebrew Temple on Skinker Boulevard (currently home to the Library and Research Center of the Missouri History Museum) and the beautiful clubhouse at Westwood Country Club on Conway Road near Ballas Road.

UNITED HEBREW TEMPLE, 1925

This page: Westwood Country Club, 1927, front (top) and living room (bottom)
Facing page: Aeolian Company, St. Louis, 1928, front (top) and interior (bottom)

ABOVE: DONNELLY MORTUARY, CLAYTON, 1932. BELOW: CLAYTON CITY HALL, 1930

ABOVE: CLAYTON NATIONAL BANK, 1930S. BELOW: CANDLE-LIGHT HOUSE, RICHMOND HEIGHTS, MISSOURI, 1937.

Above: Hillcrest Country Club, Oakville, Missouri, date unknown. Below: St. Agnes Home, Kirkwood, 1937

APPENDICES

TIMELINE

1890   Architect Gale Henderson is born in St. James, Missouri.

1893   Architects Raymond Maritz and William Ridgely Young are born; Maritz in St. Louis and Young in Louisville, Kentucky.

1895   Architect Rime Dusard is born in St. Louis.

1913   Young works as a draftsman at Mauran, Russell & Crowell.

1914   Young designs one of his first houses, for his sister on Longfellow Boulevard.

1915   The partnership of Maritz & Henderson constructs its first houses in St. Louis. Maritz heads to France as a World War I volunteer.

1918   Young leaves for France as a second lieutenant in the army.

1919   Maritz returns from the war and marries Frances Duffett. He continues his partnership with Henderson; the offices move to the Chemical Building.

1920   Henderson leaves the partnership; Young becomes Maritz's new partner.

1921   Young marries Elizabeth Nulsen.

1924   Maritz and Young become members of the American Institute of Architects (AIA).

1927   Dusard graduates from Washington University in St. Louis.

1929   The firm publishes *A Monograph of the Work of Maritz & Young*, Volume One.

1930   The firm publishes *A Monograph of the Work of Maritz & Young*, Volume Two.

1934   Rime Dusard joins the partnership.

1939   Maritz, Young & Dusard publish *Architecture & Design*, Volume Three.

1940   Young leaves the partnership.

1942   Maritz serves with the Office of Strategic Services (OSS) in Washington, D.C., before transferring to Rome to assist the British Foreign Office.

1944   Maritz returns to St. Louis and architecture. Dusard leaves the firm around this time.

1948   Ray Maritz Jr. and George Maritz join their father, and the firm changes its name to Raymond E. Maritz & Sons, Inc. William Ridgely Young dies in St. Louis at the age of fifty-five.

1962   George Maritz dies.

1966   Rime Dusard dies in St. Louis.

1969   Gale Henderson dies in St. Louis at the age of seventy-eight.

1973   Raymond Maritz dies in St. Louis at seventy-nine years old. Ray Jr. takes over the firm.

2006   Ray Maritz Jr. retires and closes the office of Raymond E. Maritz & Sons.

CATALOG

This is a listing of MARITZ & HENDERSON, Maritz & Young, and Maritz, Young & Dusard projects beginning in 1915. The list is made up of original designed and constructed houses, though a few may have been renovations and additions only. Some houses are not listed because of incomplete information in the Maritz & Young files. The addresses provided were current in the year denoted, and in some cases may not be the present address. Commercial/institutional projects are also included. The **bolded** names are profiled in this book. This listing does not include the numerous commercial/institutional and residential projects done by Raymond E. Maritz & Sons after 1948.

Maritz & Henderson

1915

Gustav Bischoff Jr.	2 Forest Ridge	Clayton, MO
Herman Schnure	6127 Lindell Blvd.	St. Louis, MO
Roy Atwood	15 Southmoor Drive	Clayton, MO

1917

Roy Scholz	20 Southmoor Drive	Clayton, MO

1920

George Duffett	7038 Lindell Blvd.	University City, MO
Raymond Maritz	7308 Westmoreland Drive	University City, MO

1921

James Maritz	7314 Maryland Avenue	University City, MO
W. Ridgely Young	7305 Maryland Avenue	University City, MO
Charles Weber	7314 Westmoreland Drive	University City, MO
Harry Papin	10 Wydown Terrace	Clayton, MO
Frank Mayfield	18 Wydown Terrace	Clayton, MO

1922

John Lionberger	6357 Ellenwood Avenue	Clayton, MO
Oliver Anderson	6365 Ellenwood Avenue	Clayton, MO
Hugh Scott	6367 Ellenwood Avenue	Clayton, MO
Theodore Luck	7062 Lindell Blvd.	University City, MO
Louis Rosen	28 Southmoor Drive	Clayton, MO
Harry Block	6363 Wydown Blvd.	Clayton, MO
Louis Martin	1 Wydown Terrace	Clayton, MO
Fairfax Funsten	19 Wydown Terrace	Clayton, MO
William Moore	20 Wydown Terrace	Clayton, MO
W. B. Marston	address unknown	Shreveport, LA

1923

N. Moskovits	7069 Delmar Blvd.	University City, MO
Vincent Price	6320 Forsyth Blvd.	Clayton, MO
LeRoy Bush	6336 Forsyth Blvd.	Clayton, MO
Heman Pettengill	34 Glen Eagles Drive	Ladue, MO
Ira Stevens	1 High Downs Lane	Ladue, MO
Herbert Piou	7301 Maryland Avenue	University City, MO

Louis Mahler	39 W. Brentmoor Drive	Clayton, MO
F. Nulsen/C. McCrea	7018 Westmoreland Drive	University City, MO
Frank Nulsen	7048 Westmoreland Drive	University City, MO
Raymond Stahlberg	7204 Westmoreland Drive	University City, MO
Walter Johnson	14 Wydown Terrace	Clayton, MO
W. Ridgely Young	27 Wydown Terrace	Clayton, MO

1924

Edmund O'Donnell	6301 Alexander Drive	Clayton, MO
Morris Schweig	570 Bedford Avenue	University City, MO
Gustav Biston	6434 Cecil Avenue	Clayton, MO
E. Rawlings	6970 Cornell Avenue	University City, MO
Sidney Baer	901 Kent Road	Ladue, MO
Arthur Dickie	640 Polo Drive	Clayton, MO
Edmund Campbell	536 Purdue Avenue	University City, MO
Samuel Plant	15 St. Andrews Drive	Ladue, MO
Mahlon Wallace Jr.	100 Sunningdale Drive	Ladue, MO
S. Watts Smyth	16 W. Brentmoor Drive	Clayton, MO
Woodson Woods	18 W. Brentmoor Drive	Clayton, MO
John O'Fallon Jr.	38 W. Brentmoor Drive	Clayton, MO
Gilbert Tuffli	7339 Westmoreland Drive	University City, MO
Elizabeth B. Conant	6 Wydown Terrace	Clayton, MO
Mary Scullin Green	9 Wydown Terrace	Clayton, MO
Julia Klein	15 Wydown Terrace	Clayton, MO

1925

Oscar Buder	8 Carrswold Drive	Clayton, MO
Francis Muckerman	6445 Cecil Avenue	Clayton, MO
Gustav Riesmeyer Jr.	6454 Cecil Avenue	Clayton, MO
T. Van Scholski	56 Crestwood Drive	Clayton, MO
John Hill	7266 Creveling Drive	University City, MO
George Taylor	6352 Forsyth Blvd.	Clayton, MO
William Lewin	6364 Forsyth Blvd.	Clayton, MO
L. Guy Blackmer	6372 Forsyth Blvd.	Clayton, MO

Leo Rassieur	2 Southmoor Drive	Clayton, MO
Morris Rosenthal	5 University Lane	Clayton, MO
Ralph Weil	7 University Lane	Clayton, MO
Ralph Bixby	11 Upper Ladue Road	Ladue, MO
Jerome Schotten	25 W. Brentmoor Drive	Clayton, MO
Kenneth Davis	37 W. Brentmoor Drive	Clayton, MO
William Schock	12 Wydown Terrace	Clayton, MO
Clark Gamble	26 Wydown Terrace	Clayton, MO
United Hebrew Temple	225 S. Skinker Blvd.	Clayton, MO

1926

Dr. Max Myer	6409 Ellenwood Avenue	Clayton, MO
William Scudder	6304 Fauquier Drive	Clayton, MO
Edwin Meissner	6244 Forsyth Blvd.	Clayton, MO
Harvey Hutchins	7287 Greenway Avenue	University City, MO
A. von Gontard	2845 Lindbergh Blvd.	Huntleigh, MO
Louis Monheimer	5795 Lindell Blvd.	St. Louis, MO
Morris Corn	5855 Lindell Blvd.	St. Louis, MO
Frank Mayfield	300 S. McKnight Road	Ladue, MO
Theodore Moreno	24 West Brentmoor Drive	Clayton, MO
Paul Lungstras	25 Wydown Terrace	Clayton, MO

1927

Edith Schofield	24 Carrswold Drive	Clayton, MO
Edwin Meyer	6226 Forsyth Blvd.	Clayton, MO
Henry Friedman	6408 Forsyth Blvd.	Clayton, MO
Oliver Anderson	9530 Ladue Road	Ladue, MO
Arnold Stifel	9750 Ladue Road	Ladue, MO
M. E. Esherwood	Oak Knoll	Belleville, IL
Clifton McMillan	11 St. Andrews Drive	Ladue, MO
William Moulton	26 W. Brentmoor Drive	Clayton, MO
Walter Hecker	31 W. Brentmoor Drive	Clayton, MO
Westwood Country Club	11801 Conway Road	St. Louis, MO

1928

Richard Waltke	3 Carrswold Drive	Clayton, MO
George Tom Murphy	22 Carrswold Drive	Clayton, MO
Horace Culling	8 Crestwood Drive	Clayton, MO
Eugene Erker	24 Crestwood Drive	Clayton, MO
A. J. Levy	32 Crestwood Drive	Clayton, MO
W. J. Schminke	2 Fair Oaks Drive	Ladue, MO
Dr. Adolph Enderle	1030 Hampton Park Drive	Richmond Heights, MO
Alexander Bischoff	750 Kent Road	Ladue, MO
Wade Childress	17 Ridgetop Street	Richmond Heights, MO
Herbert Phillips	25 Ridgetop Street	Richmond Heights, MO
Name unknown	26 Ridgetop Street	Richmond Heights, MO
Name unknown	28 Ridgetop Street	Richmond Heights, MO
Name unknown	31 Ridgetop Street	Richmond Heights, MO
Donaldson Lambert	4 St. Andrews Drive	Ladue, MO
George Murch	520 Warren Avenue	University City, MO
William Moydell	110 Overlook Court	Imperial, MO
Aeolian Company	1004 Olive Street	St. Louis, MO
Bridlespur Hunt Club	1 Squires Lane	Huntleigh, MO

1929

Lulu Engler	111 Aberdeen Place	Clayton, MO
Eugene Nims	Bee Tree Park	Oakville, MO
Albert Keller	4 Carrswold Drive	Clayton, MO
James Harris	10 Carrswold Drive	Clayton, MO
Lewis Jackson	16 Carrswold Drive	Clayton, MO
Henry Whiteside	17 Carrswold Drive	Clayton, MO
Harry Carson	25 Carrswold Drive	Clayton, MO
Morton Jourdan	6121 Lindell Blvd.	St. Louis, MO
Frank Alewel	6145 Lindell Blvd.	St. Louis, MO
William Lawler	13 Overbrook Drive	Ladue, MO
Edwin Nugent	15 Pine Valley Drive	Ladue, MO
John Latzer	28 W. Brentmoor Drive	Clayton, MO

George Bayle	7390 Westmoreland Drive	University City, MO
Louis Rosen	5 E. Ballas Road	Frontenac, MO

1930

Peters-Lauman	9 Carrswold Drive	Clayton, MO
David Woods	12 Carrswold Drive	Clayton, MO
Henry Brinckwirth	23 Carrswold Drive	Clayton, MO
E. L. Bakewell	Denny Road (Lindbergh)	Ladue, MO
James Nelson	2 Dromara Road	Ladue, MO
Conrad Pfimmer	56 Fair Oaks Drive	Ladue, MO
Percy Orthwein	2701 Lindbergh Blvd.	Huntleigh, MO
Orville Livingston	907 South Warson Road	Ladue, MO
Frank Ackerman	7384 Westmoreland Drive	University City, MO
Homer Fry	address unknown	Edwardsville, IL
Clayton City Hall	10 N. Bemiston	Clayton, MO

1931

W. Palmer Clarkson	26 Carrswold Drive	Clayton, MO
A. Dehlendorf	19 Fordyce Lane	Ladue, MO

1932

Donnelly Mortuary	3840 Lindell Blvd.	Clayton, MO

1933

Louis Atkin	12 St. Andrews Drive	Ladue, MO

Maritz, Young & Dusard

1934

Philip Platt Smith	28 Upper Ladue Road	Ladue, MO
Charles Meyer	address unknown	St. Joseph, MO

1935

C. R. Castrillon	151 Linden Avenue	Clayton, MO
Paul Bakewell	2021 S. Warson Road	Ladue, MO
Leo Carton	12 Squires Lane	Huntleigh, MO

1936

Wendell Berry	20 Fordyce Lane	Ladue, MO
Fred Hermann	10080 Litzsinger Road	Ladue, MO
T. Lewin	2 Terryhill Lane	St. Louis, MO
E. Schweich	5 Terryhill Lane	St. Louis, MO

1937

Robert Arthur	14 Carrswold Drive	Clayton, MO
Candle-Light House	7800 Clayton Road	Richmond Heights, MO
St. Agnes Home	10341 Manchester Road	Kirkwood, MO

1938

E. O'Conner	13 Countryside Lane	Frontenac, MO
Gustave Boehmer	9945 Old Chatham	Ladue, MO
Albert Stannard	500 S. Mason Road	Creve Coeur, MO
Manistee Salt Company	address unknown	Manistee, MI

1939

Bernard Klippel	52 Fair Oaks Drive	Ladue, MO
D. H. Kreutzer	address unknown	Mexico, MO
Ambruster Mortuary	6633 Clayton Road	Clayton, MO

1940

Hamblett Grigg	4 Berkshire Drive	Richmond Heights, MO
Arthur Shugg	16 Clermont Lane	Ladue, MO
J. S. McMillan	2 Greenbriar Drive	Ladue, MO
Robert Alexander	14 Woodcliffe Road	Ladue, MO

1941

Ralph Teich	17 Ellsworth Lane	Ladue, MO
Zion Evangelical Church	address unknown	Litchfield, IL

No Year

H. Harker	18 Clermont Lane	Ladue, MO
Roy Siegel	Deacon Drive	Huntleigh, MO
Richard Waltke	2015 S. Warson Road	Ladue, MO
Edmund O'Donnell	9325 Ladue Road	Ladue, MO
Frederick Meyer	6065 Lindell Blvd.	St. Louis, MO
Clarence Curby	4 Washington Terrace	St. Louis, MO
Hillcrest Country Club	Fine Road	Oakville, MO
Clayton National Bank	7817 Forsyth Blvd.	Clayton, MO
Western Military Acad.	address unknown	Alton, IL

GLOSSARY

ASHLAR: A stone pattern of large blocks cut with even faces and square edges.

BARREL VAULT: A long cylindrical ceiling arch.

CONICAL: Shaped like a cone, such as a turret roof.

CORBEL: Masonry projecting from a wall, supporting a cornice above.

CRENELLATION: A rampart constructed around the top of castle walls with regular gaps used for defense purposes.

DIAPER: A projecting diagonal brickwork design.

DORMER: A structure projecting above a sloping roof, containing an opening.

DOVECOTE: A box structure with compartments for nesting doves.

FENESTRATION: The window arrangement in a wall.

FINIAL: A crowning ornament, such as an obelisk.

FLEMISH BOND: An ornamental style of bricklaying.

GABLE: The triangular end wall below a sloping roof from the eaves to the ridge.

GOTHIC ARCH: An arch ending in a point instead of a keystone.

HARD BURNT HEADERS: Brick rotated ninety degrees to expose the end, used to create various decorative patterns in a wall including contrast in color tones through varied firing.

LINTEL: A horizontal member above an opening, supporting the load above.

ORIEL: A bay window supported upon a corbel, usually of stone.

PALLADIAN: Design based on a classical style in architecture from the work of Andrea Palladio.

PORTE-COCHERE: A covered structure extending from the entrance of a building over a driveway, sheltering both vehicles and passengers.

QUOINS: Large stones or brickwork at the corners of a building.

SOFFIT: The underside of the overhang stretching from the wall to the gutter board.

VOUSSOIRS: The wedge-shaped stones creating an arched opening.

WAINSCOT: Marble or wood paneling on the lower part of a wall.

ACKNOWLEDGMENTS

WE, THE AUTHORS, SPENT A COMBINED thirty-six years working for Raymond E. Maritz & Sons Architects, descendant firm of Maritz & Young. It was there that we first became familiar with the extraordinary catalog of residences designed by Maritz & Young.

The authors wish to thank the individuals and institutions that helped us produce this book. First, our gratitude to the Missouri History Museum and our editor, Lauren Mitchell, for producing a book beyond our expectations. St. Louis County preservation historian Esley Hamilton was the first person we contacted about writing the book. His extensive knowledge and information about St. Louis architecture, in particular the residences of Maritz & Young, was of great help in getting this project off the ground. His work in reviewing the manuscript is deeply appreciated. We want to thank the staff at the Washington University Department of Special Collections, University Archives, where the architectural drawings of Maritz & Young are stored. They were kind and patient during our numerous visits and requests; we're especially grateful to archives assistant Miranda Rectenwald. Thank you to the many people at the St. Louis County Libraries and the Missouri History Museum Archives who helped track down material, especially Dennis Northcott of the History Museum who assisted with the Elizabeth Young diaries. Thanks to Joseph Ledgerwood and Richard Squires for submitting images for the book, as well as Patrick Sullivan of the Home Builders Association of St. Louis & Eastern Missouri.

Descendants of both the architects and the homeowners have assisted us with information and/or photographs. Their contributions are greatly appreciated. They include: Deborah Earthman (Rime Dusard), Anton Brinckwirth (Henry Brinckwirth), Mr. & Mrs. Peter von Gontard (Adalbert von Gontard), the Orthwein Family (Percy Orthwein), Lisa Hughes and Mr. & Mrs. G. David Stifel (Arnold Stifel), and John Corn (Morris Corn). Stephen Robbins of Grand Junction, Colorado, graciously provided information about his father, photographer LeRoy Robbins. Special thanks go to W. Ridgely Young's daughter, Helon Lortz, and her daughter, Laura Edge, both of Greenville, South Carolina, who provided the only photographs of Ridgely Young and his wife, Elizabeth. This book would not have been possible without the support of Raymond Maritz Jr., the authors' former employer, who provided family photographs and remembrances about his father and his work.

Kevin Amsler wants also to thank his nephew Jerry Amsler for assisting with newspaper research and his wife, Vickie, for researching material, proofreading the manuscript, and offering suggestions.

—Kevin Amsler and L. John Schott, AIA

Photograph Credits

Maritz & Young, Inc., *A Monograph of the Work of Maritz & Young*, Volume One, 1929: 17 left, 28 all except detail, 30 both, 31 both, 42 big, 43 top left and right, 52 both, 53 bottom, 74 top, 75 top and bottom right, 79, 80 bottom, 95 bottom, 96 both, 100 both, 101 both, 105, 106 both, 107 both, 108, 109, 110 both, 112 both, 113 both, 120, 121 both, 122 top, 139, 140 top, 141, 146 both, 147 both, 154 top, 169 both

Maritz & Young, Inc., *A Monograph of the Work of Maritz & Young*, Volume Two, 1930: 22, 23, 36, 37 top, 44 both, 45, 46 bottom, 47 both, 51 top, 58, 59 bottom, 60 both, 61, 63 both, 64 both, 69 both, 75 bottom left, 80 top, 93, 94 all, 97, 98 both, 99, 115, 116, 117, 127 top, 128, 129, 130 both, 131, 133 top, 135, 136 top, 137, 138, 142 bottom, 149 both, 156, 161, 162 both, 167 both, 168 both, 176 both, 177 both, 180 top

Architecture and Design: Maritz, Young & Dusard, Volume Three, 1939: 16, 17 right, 21, 24, 49, 57 top, 66 top, 76 both, 77, 78 top, 82 bottom, 86 both, 144, 158 both, 159, 160 both, 165, 170 both, 171 both, 178 both, 179 both, 180 bottom

Maritz & Young Collection, University Archives, Department of Special Collections, Washington University Libraries: 9, 12 bottom, 28 detail, 33, 35 both, 41, 43 bottom, 46 top, 50, 51 bottom, 53 top, 54, 56 both, 57 bottom, 59 top, 70, 71, 72 both drawings, 74 bottom, 78 bottom, 81, 82 top, 83 bottom, 84 top, 87 both, 88 both, 102 top and right, 118, 119 both, 122 bottom, 126, 127 bottom, 132, 134, 136 bottom, 140 bottom, 142 top, 145, 151, 163 bottom

Kevin Amsler/L. John Schott: 8 bottom, 34, 55, 84 bottom, 102 bottom, 104, 114, 164

Anton Brinckwirth: 65, 66 portrait, 66 bottom, 67 both

Deborah Earthman: 18

Esley Hamilton: 40

The Hatchet, Washington University yearbook, 1914: 12 inset

Lisa Hughes and Mr. & Mrs. G. David Stifel: 143 both

Helon Young Lortz, Laura Edge: 15 both

Raymond Maritz Jr.: 8 top, 10, 13 both

Missouri History Museum: 14, 37 bottom, 42 inset, 72 inset, 83 inset, 85, 90, 92, 95 inset, 133 inset, 163 top, 175

Modern Homes: Their Design & Construction, 1930: 32

Orthwein Family: 157

Stephen Robbins: 38

Richard Squires: 103

Mr. & Mrs. Peter von Gontard: 153, 154 bottom, 155 all

BIBLIOGRAPHY

Amsler, Kevin. *Final Resting Place: The Lives and Deaths of Famous St. Louisans*. St. Louis: Virginia Publishing, 2006.

Architecture & Design: Maritz, Young & Dusard. 3, no. 13 (November 1939).

Architectural Record, April 1930.

Bry, Charlene. *Ladue Found: Celebrating 100 Years of the City's Rural-to-Regal Past*. St. Louis: Virginia Publishing, 2011.

Conard, Howard L., ed. *Encyclopedia of the History of Missouri: A Compendium of History and Biography for Ready Reference*. Vol. 3. New York: The Southern History Company, 1901.

Day, Judith Lang. "The American Gardens of Lotawana Nims." *Spritsail* 8, no. 1 (1994).

Elizabeth Nulsen Young Diaries, 1917–1976, Missouri History Museum Archives.

Encyclopedia Britannica Online, 2012, s.v. "WPA Federal Art Project."

Fitzgerald, Gerry, ed. *Maritz & Young, Inc., A Monograph of Their Work*. 2 vols. St. Louis: Blackwell-Wielandy, 1929–1930.

"Forsyth School Purchases Home," *Clayton Word*, November 2, 1995.

Fox, Elana V. *Inside the World's Fair of 1904: Exploring the Louisiana Purchase Exposition*. Vol. 1. Bloomington, IN: 1st Books Library, 2003.

Fox, Tim, ed. *Where We Live: A Guide to St. Louis Communities*. St. Louis: Missouri Historical Society Press, 1995.

Gass, Mary Henderson, Jean Fahey Eberle, and Judith Phelps Little. *Parkview: A St. Louis Urban Oasis, 1905–2005*. St. Louis: Virginia Publishing, 2005.

Gill, McCune. *The St. Louis Story: Library of American Lives*. St. Louis: Historical Record Association, 1952.

Gould's St. Louis City Directory. St. Louis: Polk-Gould Directory Company, 1916, 1929, 1930, 1932, 1935, 1938, 1939, 1940, 1946, 1947, 1948, 1952, 1955, 1958.

Gould's St. Louis City Red-Blue Book. St. Louis: Polk-Gould Directory Company, 1921.

Hagen, Harry. *This Is Our St. Louis*. St. Louis: Knight Publishing Company, 1970.

Hamilton, Esley. "Forsyth Avenue: A Proper Setting for a University." Report, 1996.

____. "Historic Inventory." Report for St. Louis County Parks & Recreation, 1980–1994.

____. "National Register of Historic Places Inventory—Carrswold and Brentmoor Park/Forest Ridge, and Forsyth/Wydown Nomination Form." 1982 and 1988.

Harris, Cyril Manton. *American Architecture: An Illustrated Encyclopedia*. New York: W. W. Norton, 1998.

Hatchet, The (Washington University yearbook). Vols. 9, 15, 22, and 24 (1912).

Hernon, Peter, and Terry Ganey. *Under the Influence: The Unauthorized Story of the Anheuser-Busch Dynasty*. New York: Simon & Schuster, 1991.

"Home Is Link to Area's Past." *St. Louis Post-Dispatch*, August 18, 1991.

Kargau, Ernest D. *Mercantile, Industrial and Professional St. Louis*. St. Louis: Nixon-Jones Printing Company, 1902[?].

Kimbrough, Mary. *St. Louis Country Club: The First 100 Years 1892–1992*. St. Louis: St. Louis Country Club, 1992.

Knoedelseder, William. *Bitter Brew: The Rise and Fall of Anheuser-Busch and America's Kings of Beer*. New York: HarperCollins, 2012.

Leonard, John W., ed. *The Book of St. Louisans*. St. Louis: *St. Louis Republic*, 1906.

Leonard, Mary Delach, and Melinda Leonard. *Clayton, Missouri: An Urban Story*. St. Louis: Reedy Press, 2012.

Little, Judy. *University City Landmarks and Historic Places*. University City, MO: The Commission, 1997.

Lortz, Helon Young. Interview with Kevin Amsler, May 17, 2012.

Loughlin, Caroline, and Catherine Anderson. *Forest Park*. Columbia, MO: University of Missouri Press / Junior League of St. Louis, 1986.

Maritz & Young Collection, Architectural Drawings and Photographs. Washington University Libraries, University Archives, Department of Special Collections.

Maritz, Ray, Jr. Interview with Kevin Amsler, February 24, 2012.

McCue, George, and Frank Peters. *A Guide to the Architecture of St. Louis*. Columbia, MO: University of Missouri Press, 1989.

Millstein, Cydney, and Carol Grove. *Houses of Missouri 1870–1940*. New York: Acanthus Press, 2008.

Missouri State Archives Death Certificate Database. St. Louis County Libraries.

Modern Homes: Their Design & Construction. New York: American Builder Publishing Company, 1930.

Necrology: Volumes E, F, 16, 20, 23, 29.

Parish, James Robert, and Steven Whitney. *Vincent Price Unmasked: A Biography*. New York: Drake Publishers, 1974.

Price, Victoria. *Vincent Price: A Daughter's Biography*. New York: St. Martin's Press, 1999.

Primm, James Neal. *Lion of the Valley: St. Louis, Missouri*. St. Louis: Missouri Historical Society Press, 1998.

"Ralph Weil, Clothing Firm Chairman, Dies." *St. Louis Globe-Democrat*, July 3, 1952.

"Raymond E. Maritz: An Appreciation." *Newsletter of the Missouri Valley Chapter, Society of Architectural Historians* 3, no. 2 (1997).

Robbins, Stephen. Interview with Kevin Amsler, November 6, 2012.

Shepley, Carol Ferring. *Movers and Shakers, Scalawags and Suffragettes: Tales from Bellefontaine Cemetery.* St. Louis: Missouri History Museum, 2008.

Steinbreder, John. *Golf Courses of the U.S. Open.* Dallas: Taylor Publishing Company, 1996.

St. Louis Exclusive Social Register, The. St. Louis: O. L. Hopper & J. D. Normile, 1934.

St. Louisans You Should Know. St. Louis: Welcome Inn, 1935.

Terry, Dickson. *Clayton: A History.* Clayton, MO: City of Clayton, 1976.

Thomas, William. *History of St. Louis County Missouri.* St. Louis: S. J. Clarke Publishing, 1911.

Toft, Carolyn Hewes. *St. Louis: Landmarks & Historic Districts.* St. Louis: Landmarks Association of St. Louis, 2002.

Toft, Carolyn Hewes, Esley Hamilton, and Mary Henderson Gass. *The Way We Came: A Century of the AIA in St. Louis.* St. Louis: Patrice Press, 1991.

Tracy, Walter. *Men Who Make St. Louis the City of Opportunity.* St. Louis: Author, 1927.

25th Anniversary Progress Club, International Shoe Company, 1917–1942. St. Louis, 1942.

U.S. Census Office. *Census of the United States.* Washington, D.C.: National Archives and Records Service, 1920, 1930.

"W. Ridgely Young Funeral Services to be Private." *St. Louis Post-Dispatch*, December 2, 1948.

Who's Who in St. Louis. St. Louis: Civic Union of St. Louis, 1930–1931.

World War I Biography and Service Records: Persons Who Enlisted in St. Louis City and County. St. Louis: Missouri Historical Society, 1994.

Young, Andrew D., and Eugene G. Provenzo Jr. *The History of the St. Louis Car Company, "Quality Shops."* San Diego: Howell-North Books, 1978.